Political Religion

Sermons On The Gospel Readings
For Sundays After Pentecost
(Middle Third)

Cycle A

Wayne Brouwer

CSS Publishing Company, Inc., Lima, Ohio

POLITICAL RELIGION

Copyright © 2007 by
CSS Publishing Company, Inc.
Lima, Ohio

All rights reserved. No part of this publication may be reproduced in any manner whatsoever without the prior permission of the publisher, except in the case of brief quotations embodied in critical articles and reviews. Inquiries should be addressed to: Permissions, CSS Publishing Company, Inc., 517 South Main Street, Lima, Ohio 45804.

Some scripture quotations are from the *New Revised Standard Version of the Bible*, copyright 1989 by the Division of Christian Education of the National Council of the Churches of Christ in the USA. Used by permission.

Some scripture quotations are from the Holy Bible, New International Version. Copyright © 1973, 1978, 1984 International Bible Society. Used by permission of Zondervan Bible Publishers. All rights reserved.

For more information about CSS Publishing Company resources, visit our website at www.csspub.com or email us at csr@csspub.com or call (800) 241-4056.

Cover design by Barbara Spencer
ISBN-13: 978-0-7880-2409-9
ISBN-10: 0-7880-2409-0   PRINTED IN USA

*To the people
of Harderwyk Ministries
who shared the journey
for eleven years*

Table Of Contents

Preface — 7

Proper 12 — 9
Pentecost 10
Ordinary Time 17
    Why We Need The Pledge Of Allegiance
    Matthew 13:31-33, 44-52

Proper 13 — 19
Pentecost 11
Ordinary Time 18
    Hunger And Politics
    Matthew 14:13-21

Proper 14 — 27
Pentecost 12
Ordinary Time 19
    Ecological Politics
    Matthew 14:22-33

Proper 15 — 35
Pentecost 13
Ordinary Time 20
    Religious Balkanization
    Matthew 15:(10-20) 21-28

Proper 16 — 43
Pentecost 14
Ordinary Time 21
    Mistaken Identity
    Matthew 16:13-20

Proper 17 53
Pentecost 15
Ordinary Time 22
    The Road No One Wants To Travel
    Matthew 16:21-28

Proper 18 65
Pentecost 16
Ordinary Time 23
    Personal Politics
    Matthew 18:15-20

Proper 19 75
Pentecost 17
Ordinary Time 24
    Political Pardon
    Matthew 18:21-35

Proper 20 89
Pentecost 18
Ordinary Time 25
    Why Is God Unfair?
    Matthew 20:1-16

Proper 21 99
Pentecost 19
Ordinary Time 26
    A Career In The Kingdom
    Matthew 21:23-32

Proper 22 111
Pentecost 20
Ordinary Time 27
    Kingdoms In Conflict
    Matthew 21:33-46

Preface

One cannot read the gospel of Matthew without quickly running into the kingdom of heaven. Jesus is born of royal stock (ch. 1), announced to the world as a supranational king (ch. 2), declared kingdom business as his message (ch. 4), assumed the allegiance of others to him as a rightful expression (ch. 9), and commands the powers available only to a king (ch. 10). He engages in conversations that suppose his royal identity (ch. 12), speaks openly about the character of the kingdom (ch. 13), and reveals himself as king (ch. 17). He legislates the moral ethos of the dominion (chs. 18-19), is identified and received by others as king (ch. 21), is challenged about his kingship (ch. 27), and announces his royal rule (ch. 28). The kingdom of heaven is clearly a major theme of Jesus' identity and its expressions through the gospel of Matthew.

We who live in democratic societies twenty centuries after Jesus' life in Palestine read the words "kingdom of heaven" and hear sermons about Jesus' teachings, but we typically theologize them until we de-politicize their meaning. We do not live with kings or royalty. They are odd anachronisms of bygone eras in European and Asian histories, which have never functioned in North American society. So we think that our "separation of church and state" means religion has little to do with politics. At most, it may be something which informs the consciences of people who then might lobby to enact certain forms of legislation that salve our uneasy consciences about our social obligations. But religion as such is or ought to be apolitical.

We need to clean out our ears and take the pious cataracts off our eyes in order to hear and see again the very essential political character of the religion of Jesus. Jesus did not assume he could speak to and about the political affairs of his day; he assumed he had a right to declare the true character of politics precisely because he spoke religiously. Any power is religious power. Any kingdom is a reflection of or a challenge to the one real kingdom. Religion is political or it is not religion at all.

In the pages that follow, something of the political religion of Matthew's gospel reemerges. Perhaps we can set aside our spiritual reductionisms enough to be captured by a cause and a king who deserves our attention and allegiance.

— Wayne Brouwer

**Proper 12
Pentecost 10
Ordinary Time 17
Matthew 13:31-33, 44-52**

Why We Need The Pledge Of Allegiance

When I was in high school, a new music teacher came to town. He was fresh out of college and full of ambition. But here he was, stuck in a very rural community where people didn't put up with (as they called it) "long-haired music," either from the Beatles or Beethoven.

Still, he was determined to teach us good music. We were going to sing selections from Handel's *Messiah* for our Christmas concert. Most of us had never heard of George Frideric Handel, and when we first tried to sight-read through the selections we became convinced we didn't like his music. It was too hard, too complicated. More than that, Handel wouldn't allow us to sing simple harmonies; no, he created different parts for each voice, and we in the bass section weren't able to hide all our typical mistakes when Handel and our new director demanded that we sing alone.

Our fearless leader did his best, but half-way to Christmas, it was obvious that we were all losing: We in the choir had lost our places, he as director and new teacher on the block was about to lose face, and Handel had long ago lost interest in all of us. Still, we had gone too far to turn back, and with a grace we didn't feel we stumbled through the first part of our concert. Our parents smiled politely, while our little sisters and brothers squirmed restlessly. Some of our grandparents with hearing problems even managed to smile.

Finally, after too many minutes of painful lapses and a competition between ourselves and the piano, which neither won, we came to our last section, the one we knew best. As we raced through the opening lines, a few people actually stood up! At first we thought they were walking out on us, but they just stood there beaming until we had shouted our last "King of Kings, and Lord of Lords! Hal - le - lu - jah!"

Later, of course, we learned why these few fearless folks had risen to the occasion. When the German prince, George II, became king of Great Britain, he had a special fondness for Handel's music. At the premier concert of the *Messiah* in 1743, the king and the crowds were deeply moved by the glory and grace of the masterpiece. When the musicians swelled the "Hallelujah Chorus" and thundered those mighty words "... and he shall reign for ever and ever!" King George, whose English wasn't all that great, jumped to his feet thinking that they sang about him.

The whole crowd, naturally, followed suit, although they were standing more out of ceremonial habit, and thinking about a different king. Since that day, though, people have continued to stand for the "Hallelujah Chorus" to worship the glory of God whose kingdom shall know no end.

Rethinking The Kingdom

But what kind of kingdom is it? How, among the many nasty dictatorships and the autocratic tyrannies and the changing number of troubled democracies of this world, do we think about the kingdom of God, especially when it plays such a large part in the teaching of the Bible? Matthew 13, for instance, is a profound collection of parables by Jesus whose primary focus is the kingdom of heaven. Writing to a primarily Jewish-Christian community, Matthew honors the devout tradition of minimizing public use of the name of God by using the term "kingdom of heaven." Elsewhere among the gospels and throughout the New Testament the equivalent idea, "kingdom of God," is dominant.

Some of us have the notion that the kingdom of God is primarily a secret and personal rule of God in individual hearts. God is no earthly ruler whose fortunes are dictated by the latest research poll. His name won't appear on the ballots when we vote in November. *Time* magazine is not likely to declare God as a list topper in one of its annual collections of "most powerful leaders in the world."

God doesn't have his own political party, though a few small groups attempt to lay claim to him as leader. Back in 1951, shortly before he was forced from his throne by a military coup, King Farouk of Egypt confided bitterly to British Lord Boyd-Orr, "There will soon be only five kings left — the kings of England, diamonds, hearts, spades, and clubs."

That is sometimes the way we see the kingdom of God, sifted through the world like the kings in a deck of cards. The king of heaven may have a kind of power when we play a certain game called religion, but for the most part it is a rather invisible and private authority, one held closely in your hand so no one else sees, and played as a trump card when you run out of other options.

Perhaps there is some reason for this view. Didn't Jesus himself tell Pilate, "My kingdom is not of this world"? (John 18:36 NIV). And another time, when the Pharisees came to Jesus and asked him about the kingdom of God, Jesus told them, "The kingdom of God does not come with your careful observation, nor will people say, 'Here it is,' or 'There it is,' because the kingdom of God is within you" (Luke 17:20-2 NIV). Even the apostle Paul seemed to echo that when he wrote about the rule of God as being "in your heart" (Romans 10:8).

Another thought we sometimes have about the kingdom of God is that it is really the same thing as the church. One of the great hymns puts it like this:

> *I love Thy Kingdom, Lord, the House of Thine abode;*
> *The Church our blessed Redeemer saved with His own*
> *precious blood.*

These words tie the kingdom of God directly to the church. While national governments may wield temporal power of armies and economies, the church claims spiritual power and a moral sway over values and behavior. This view sees the world in two parts: a "secular" life of week days and business and family and school, and a "sacred" life of the church and spirit which sneaks in now and again like the weekend "religion" pages of the newspaper.

A third view of the kingdom of God reacts strongly to the individualism and private spirituality of a privatized religion, and sees in Jesus' words a socially transforming message. In 1917, while the kingdoms of this world were at war, while revolution stalked Russia and set up a dictatorship of the proletariat, while labor strikes were sweeping across North America, Walter Rauschenbusch delivered four addresses at the Yale School of Religion. He had been pastor at the Second German Baptist Church in a suburb of New York City politely called "Hell's Kitchen." He had seen children working fourteen-hour shifts in dark and dirty factories. He watched pregnant women hemorrhage to death while standing at their industrial posts. He said funeral prayers for men who died in tragic accidents, whose families would be turned out into streets at the loss of income and lack of insurance or pensions.

He was supposed to preach the love of God, the grace of God, the providence of God from his pulpit, week after week, Sunday after Sunday. But where was God on Monday, while the bosses treated their workers like slaves? Where was God on Tuesday, when pollution took the life of a sickly child? Was the gospel limited to things "sacred"? Was salvation only for people's souls, while their bodies could rot in Hell's Kitchen?

Rauschenbusch searched the scriptures and prayed as Jesus taught, "Thy kingdom come!" Then he challenged Christians to look for a kingdom that was bigger than the church, a kingdom that stepped into the world on Monday and organized labor unions, that fought political battles on Tuesday, and demanded social justice on Wednesday. He called for people of God who took a piece of heaven and set it to grow here on earth.

A fourth possibility, when we look for a way to read these parables of the kingdom, is that Jesus is primarily focusing our attention on the future, and keeping our eyes trained toward the skies. We know that some day the Lord who spoke these parables will come back again, and then the fullness of his kingdom will become a glorious reality. Now, however, we live in the kingdom of Satan, the prince of this age, the ruler of the powers of darkness, as Paul put it. So we hide ourselves into our corners and protect our little ones as best we can, until someday we will see Jesus return and then we will live in his kingdom. The old gospel song testified to it like this:

> *This world is not my home, I'm just a-passin' through;*
> *My treasures are laid up, somewhere beyond the blue.*
> *The angels beckon me from heaven's open door*
> *And I can't feel at home in this world anymore.*

An All-Encompassing Citizenship

We have all been touched by each of these views of the kingdom of heaven. Yet today, as we read Jesus' parables again, it is important to hear the undercurrent of what he is saying. First of all, the idea of "kingdom" implies citizenship, or at least allegiance to a governing authority. This is Jesus' theme in his parable of the treasures (Matthew 13:44-46). Among the pieces of properties that we collect in this life, says Jesus, we may someday suddenly stumble upon a treasure that collects us. It possesses us. It demands allegiance from us.

It is the kind of thing that J.R.R. Tolkien tried to picture in his powerful trilogy *The Lord of the Rings*. Writing in the recovery years after World War II, Tolkien imagined what powers there are in this world that can possess peoples and nations, for good or for ill. His tale of the struggles of Middle Earth allegorically reflected the biblical idea of kingdoms in conflict.

Either, as Jesus indicates, we play games with little treasures, buying and selling them on world markets, and moving among commercial districts that hold our attraction for a while, or we are sold out to a greater power. We sell all and buy it. We give up our claims in order that we might be claimed.

Our youngest daughter was born in Nigeria while I was teaching at the Reformed Theological College in Mkar. Because the Nigerian government does not automatically grant citizenship to all who are born on its soil, Kaitlyn was truly a person without a country in her earliest days. Until I could process her existence with the United States consulate in Kaduna, she had no official identity, no traveling permissions, and no rights in society outside of our home. We took a picture of her at five days old, sleeping in my hands, and this became the photograph used on her passport for the first ten years of her life. The snapshot may have become outdated quickly as she grew through the stages of childhood, but the passport to which it was affixed declared that she belonged to the United States of America. She had rights. She had privileges. She had protection under the law. When the time came for us to leave Nigeria and travel through three continents to get back to North America, that little passport opened doors and prepared the way for her. She had never lived in the US, but the US knew her by name and kept watch over her.

So it is and more with the kingdom of heaven, according to Jesus. It becomes the badge of identification for us, as well as the symbol of our protection and care. When we choose other pearls, or dig around for treasures in our own backyards we get from them what we are looking for — things that we can possess. But when the great prize of the hidden treasure comes our way, or we stumble onto the pearl of great price, we realize that our little hordes are insufficient. It is not enough to own a piece of fading substance; we need to be owned by something which transcends our time. We need God to lay hold on us.

This is why, in many of the earliest liturgical forms for baptism, those who were newly coming into the fellowship of believers were asked if they renounced the devil and all his works. Early on, it was recognized that entering the kingdom of God was more than just adding another spiritual talisman to the mix of superstitious hex warders; it was a fundamental commitment of identity that could not be shared. No dual passports in this kingdom! The truly great treasure demands that one sell everything else. It is exclusive. And when it is purchased, it actually purchases you.

Living On A Battlefield

A second implication of Jesus' parables in this chapter is that we are under orders. Not every citizen in most realms is thereby automatically also a soldier preparing for battle. A few times in history it has been close to the truth — when the modern state of Israel was founded, for instance, and all of its neighbors made a concerted effort to drive it into the sea. Suddenly everyone was under military orders; there was no other way to survive. While this is not a typical occurrence of our citizenship experiences, it does in fact mirror the urgency of Jesus' view of the kingdom of heaven.

Certainly, of course, we have to be careful with battlefield images as we communicate Christianity. Too often our world has experienced bellicose religion in forms that have destroyed civilizations, dehumanized societies, degraded value systems, and diminished piety. We have had enough of religious groups battling for domination at the expense of God's honor and human dignity.

Yet, one cannot read both Old and New Testaments without appreciating the challenge of transformation that places citizens of the kingdom of God under orders. Jesus speaks to that in his parable of the net (Matthew 13:47-52). The kingdom of heaven is like a net that catches fish. It is not like a hook thrown carelessly into the water in case a silly fish might be stupid enough to nip at it. No, the kingdom of heaven, says Jesus, is a network of citizens who together are constantly under orders to bring in others.

Some time ago, I talked with a pastor of a large congregation in a major city. He was pleased with the worship and the ministries of his church. Everything seemed to operate with care and good taste and competence. He had the right staff in place, and they all were able to find dedicated, trained volunteers to shape a marvelous network of programs. Yet, something didn't sit right with him. In his words, it was a very, very nice church. And therein was the problem. It was a church that looked after itself so well that it had forgotten that it was under orders to be about the missionary business of the kingdom of heaven.

If people wanted wonderful worship, all they had to do was join the congregation on Sundays. If they wanted terrific children's ministries and youth programs, all they had to do was drop their sons and daughters off at the right times. If anyone wanted a little diaconal assistance, just stop by the office and a secretary would arrange for a modest handout.

But the onus was on others to come and find the church. The congregation itself had little use for going out to search for the lost and the last and the least. It had given up being a net. It had lost its marching orders. It had gained the corner on "nice" but was losing the ability to call itself church.

C. S. Lewis knew the battlefield connection underlying Christianity. He came about that insight in a very personal way. When he was nine years old, his warm and loving mother contracted cancer. Within a very short time, she was confined to bed, enduring harsh treatments, in terrible pain, and stinking because of the sores and horrible wasting of her body. At night she would cry out in anguish, and young Jack (as he was known) hid in terror under his covers. He had heard the minister say that God answers prayer, so he begged God for his mother's deliverance. But to no avail. She died gasping and screaming, and his belief in God went with her.

Years later, when as an Oxford professor he began to rationally think through the possibility of Christian belief, Lewis finally understood what was going on in his mother's painful illness. He came to see that this world is a battlefield between the kingdom of God and the powers of evil, and that Christianity was true precisely because it took this conflict seriously. The religion of the Bible was not a streamlined Santa Claus story of a jolly old grandfather figure who always brings gifts, whether you are naughty or nice. Rather, it is an acknowledgment of the struggles present in this world and the necessary reality of God's intervention. Lewis' mother died not because God didn't grant a child's wish but because the evil one had twisted God's good world in such a way that even the very cells of her body no longer worked as they should. But though healing did not come in that instant of boyish spiritual lisping, the prayers did not go unheard, and his mother was not lost forever or forgotten.

So the parable of the net reminds us of our marching orders in the kingdom of heaven. We are not saved so that we may politely pat ourselves on the back and smile at one another in the tiny corners we occupy. No, we are part of a net that seeks and engages the fish of this world who might be swimming to their own destruction.

Confidence

Finally, Jesus' stories in this chapter remind us that we are on the winning side in the battles of life. When Jesus tells the parables of the seed and the yeast (Matthew 13:31-35), he presents a picture of the kingdom of heaven that grows and dominates until it is the primary factor shaping the world. The tiny mustard seed morphs into a tree that provides a home for the birds, and the bit of yeast transforms the entire loaf until it is utterly and completely changed. And, it is important to note, these things happen rather automatically. The change takes place from within the seed, and from within the grain of yeast.

In other words, the kingdom of heaven has the winning power within itself, and invites us along on the journey. We do not create the kingdom, but the kingdom creates us. Even though it appears to be insignificant at the start, the essence of greatness and the confidence of success lies within.

Scripture is filled with testimonies to this. One in particular from the Old Testament is the scene in Jeremiah 32 where the prophet buys a field. Normally, this would seem like an ordinary transaction, just another day at the real estate office. But Jeremiah and the salesperson are both holed up inside the walls of Jerusalem, and the battering rams of Babylon's armies are pounding the gates and walls to rubble. What is more, in the prolonged siege of Jerusalem, the invading armies have killed and burned every living thing for miles, and made waste of whatever farmland there might have been in the region. Added to that is the sure promise of God, spoken through Jeremiah himself, that this time Babylon would be successful and the city, along with the temple, would be destroyed.

If there was ever a bad time to invest in real estate, this was it. The land itself was worthless, the currency inflated, the threat of destruction obvious and the future about as grim as any could be. Yet, Jeremiah buys the field. Why? Because he knew the power of the seed of the kingdom of God. He knew that God would have his way, even beyond the threat of Babylon. He knew that in spite of the waywardness of the people, God's kingdom would rise again and thrust itself to the heavens until even the Babylonian vulture would nest in its branches.

When we hear Jesus tell us about the kingdom of heaven we recover our sense of values and outcomes in the quagmire of daily events. We carry the passport of heaven. We live as those who are under orders to be and do and make a difference. And we know who writes the last chapter, because the kingdom of heaven is growing tenaciously around us in spite of reports to the contrary.

When we were very young we learned the "Pledge of Allegiance" to the flag of the United States of America. We were taught to understand and respect the symbol of our country, and to renew our commitments to its well-being. Far more significant, as Jesus reminds us in these parables, is our need as Christians to regularly and repeatedly stand together and recite the greatest pledge of allegiance of all time, and even eternity:

> *I pledge allegiance to the Christian flag and to the Savior for whose kingdom it stands. One Savior, crucified, risen, and coming again, with life and liberty for all who believe.*

Amen.

**Proper 13
Pentecost 11
Ordinary Time 18
Matthew 14:13-21**

Hunger And Politics

Yogi Berra, the great baseball player of an earlier age, was known for his unusual and creative use of the English language. In giving directions to his home, for example, he often told people, "When you come to the fork in the road, take it." His formula for success, as some heard it, was this: "Ninety percent perspiration, and the rest mostly just plain hard work." Then there was the time he went to a restaurant by himself and ordered a large pizza. The waitress asked if he would like it cut into four or eight pieces. "Better make it four," he replied. "I'm not hungry enough to eat eight."

Yogi Berra may have had a few things to learn about food service, but those who followed Jesus into the Galilean hillsides were very pleased that Jesus was able to cut five loaves and two fish into enough pieces to satisfy a huge crowd. They were certainly hungry enough to eat more than just the original seven or even Yogi Berra's famous eight.

Of course, as Matthew tells the story, he has some particular thoughts in mind which go far beyond merely the miraculous event itself. After all, he does not give as many details as John would in his later gospel — talking about the boy who brought the food, or the extended dialogue Jesus has with those who introduced the lad to their master. Here Matthew spits out the story quickly and moves right on to another miracle. But that's the way he does it, over and over again. Matthew had lived with Jesus long enough to find what others might call unusual made ordinary, and things that most considered spectacular to be almost commonplace.

But that doesn't mean Matthew is telling us about an event with no consequence. Much to the contrary, Matthew has some very important ideas he wants his readers to pick up.

Who Serves In The Wilderness?
First of all, we have to remember that Matthew is writing to a community that is primarily composed of Jewish Christians. He makes this clear in the way he opens the gospel. Most other biographies don't start out with a wander through a cemetery, but that is how we encounter Jesus here. Verses 1-17 of Matthew 1 move in stages through the memorial gardens of Israelite history, stopping briefly to read the grave markers on nearly forty sites. These are representatives of the major eras of Hebrew history, Matthew tells us.

This, of course, makes us immediately aware that Jesus enters a particular history. He does not appear without a context, like a stone skipping across a pond that happens to flit and hit in some random manner, and then dive into the pool at a chance spot. Jesus, according to Matthew, is the "son of David" and the "son of Abraham." This is quite a loaded statement, for those two great figures were called by God to establish the character of the nation of Israel. Abraham received the first great covenant promise of God when God picked him out of the crowds of Mesopotamia and sent him on a journey to what would become the promised land (Genesis 12:1-2). Out of this transforming event was born the people of Israel. Their beginnings and the name of Abraham were forever linked.

Then, generations later, the great King David was divinely assured that he would always have a son of the family ruling as king (2 Samuel 6-7). Throughout the centuries, even though the Israelites lost huge tracts of their land to foreign invaders and were diminished in numbers until only a remnant remained, they kept tracking the descendents of David. One day, they knew, a child would be born from this blood line who would reassert home rule and re-establish national hope.

So when Matthew marks Jesus' entrance into the human arena, he reminds those who own this particular portion of history that

Jesus is one of them, that Jesus came as a member of the family, and that Jesus is heir to the unique promises announced to their forebears. Moreover, Matthew goes on in chapter 1 to describe Jesus' unique birth. The child doesn't show up in the usual way, Matthew declares. For Jesus' parents it was not to be a prayed-for pregnancy in the first year after marriage, the kind that brings the family together for a big celebration party.

Instead, Mary finds herself with child in a manner and at a time that appear unquestionably scandalous: she is pregnant without Joseph's help, and begins showing before their marriage has been publicly confirmed. Embarrassment and suspicion would entirely overshadow both the baby and the family were it not for the arrival of a divine messenger who announced this as God's deliberate interruption of all their lives. While people from other traditions who read this gospel may not easily catch it, for devout Jews it was a brilliant revelation. They would immediately place this birth alongside those of Samson and Samuel, two of the greatest deliverers their history had produced. In each instance a boy was born under unusual circumstances, and on each occasion an angel came to clarify God's designs. Obviously, this child was destined for greatness, and in his wake would flow deliverance and restoration.

To make the point unmistakable, just a few lines later in chapter 2, Matthew calls to mind the ancient conspiracy of Pharaoh to get rid of the male babies in Israel by relating King Herod's plot to slay the infants of Bethlehem. While the other boys died, Jesus, like Moses, was divinely protected. Once again Matthew's Jewish Christian audience would draw out the parallel. In fact, Matthew reaffirms this comparison by relating that when Jesus began his public teachings (ch. 5) he first climbed a mountain, and then delivered an updated version of the covenant stipulations which were earlier mediated by Moses to Israel at Mount Sinai. Jesus must be the new Moses for this new age in which God's people find themselves.

In other words, Matthew wants us to know up front and all the way through that Jesus is the uniquely birthed and commissioned Messiah of the Jews. With this in mind we are helped to understand why Matthew can quickly toss off to us the story of Jesus feeding the crowds in what might appear at first to be an almost cavalier way, from our point of view. If Jesus is indeed the Messiah, as all the signs indicate, he obviously wields divine power and purpose. Therefore, if the God of ancient Israel made it a concern to feed those who came out into the wilderness to experience God's leading and provision, people in Jesus' day could expect the same thing from him. In the deserts of the Sinai Peninsula God provided manna to the hungry tribes of Israel; Jesus, as God's agent, makes sure there is food enough for the famished Jewish crowds. It's a no-brainer.

Anybody Hungry?

But that only leads us to the second and more important thing Matthew wants us to think about. Who are these people that Jesus feeds? Who would be so foolish as to go unprepared out into the wilderness running after Jesus? Why would anybody do that in the first place?

I find a clue to that in books like John Hull's autobiography, *Touching the Rock* (New York: Random House, Inc., 1992). His is both a personal story and a spiritual saga. At age seventeen, Hull began to go blind in his left eye. One day he realized that the only way he would ever see his left shoulder again would be by turning to his side and catching his reflection in the mirror with his right eye. Later the blindness spread, and eventually John's sight was gone entirely.

Hull writes that for a while he energetically tried to remember what he looked like. He thought about old photographs of himself and struggled to recall the face that peered back at him from the bathroom mirror when he shaved. After a while, though, his memory banks gave out and he couldn't remember his own face anymore.

"Who am I?" he thought, with a wash of panic. "If I don't even know my own face, who am I?"

Worse still, however, was his daughter, Lizzie's, question. She was only four years old when she asked him, "Daddy, how can a smile be between us when you can't see my face?"

It was Lizzie's curious questions that prompted Hull to write his book. He wanted to remember himself and repicture the times and circumstances that made it important and unique. More than that, he wished for Lizzie to know him in his sighted and unsighted years. His biography was a journal to restore the smiles between them.

But then, as he surveyed his life in its spiritual dimensions, Hull took his daughter's query to a level higher. "How can a smile be between us and God if we cannot see *his* face?" he asked.

As he reflected, Hull came to realize that the only way we can see God is when we take what little God gives us to work with and use it as a kind of tarnished mirror to seek out God's distant face. In other words, said Hull, we are all somewhat blinded, and we need to use things like the scriptures and the person of Jesus to help us take first steps toward making a smile happen between ourselves and God. In this, he echoed Matthew's design in writing the gospel. Those of us who did not originally stand with Jesus in that ancient wilderness are no less hungry than they were. We are all looking for meaning in our lives. To a person we are searchers on a quest for purpose or identity. The hunger is in every belly, and each of us finds ourselves in strange wilderness places as we look and seek.

But what will we find? And how will it become visible to us? Where will we see the smile between God and us? However it will happen, according to Matthew, it will be when we first believe that Jesus has what it takes to satisfy our cravings.

A friend called me one Saturday. He was a perennial student, far away from the town that shaped him, and mostly at odds with his family. There was good reason for his mother to chide and nag and scold, for my friend had lost his faith, and his parents were worried. But the more they pushed the certainty of their beliefs on him, the more he chafed and backed away. He could no longer live in the simplicity of their dogma, even if it gave them shelter and safety.

So now he wandered in the wilderness of academia, hoping in each class to find a glorious utopia or a grand dream or at least a tiny map that might point toward some secularized Holy Grail.

Every term, he called me to describe his latest faculty mentor, a true savior, finally, who was worthy of his devotion. But this Saturday, something was different. There was wistfulness in my friend's voice, and a trembling uncertainty in his words. What if there was no big picture or all-encompassing thesis or unifying meaning? What if we were tripping with stumbling paces through the wilderness and there was no limit or signpost or way out? What if he was on a quest, but there was nothing to find?

"I'm lonely," he told me, and I was left to imagine his cosmic, spiritual aloneness, a void where both heaven and hell were silent and he was left in awful communion with only his inadequate self. There was no dream here; only an incessant heart hunger kept awake by an unrelenting nightmare.

Generations ago, George Herbert penned a brilliant picture of the aching in each of our souls. In his poem, "The Pulley," he portrayed God at the moment of creation, sprinkling his new human creature with treasures kept in a jar beside him. These were God's finest resources, given now as gifts to the crown of his universe: beauty, wisdom, honor, pleasure.... All were scattered liberally in the genetic recipe of our kind.

When the jar of God's treasures was nearly empty, God put the lid on it. The angels wondered why God did not finish the human concoction, leaving one great resource still in its container. This last quality, God told the angels, is "rest." But God would not grant that divine treasure to the human race.

Restless Spirituality

The angels, of course, asked why. Herbert was ready with the divine answer regarding the best mix for the human spirit.

> *Let him be rich and weary, that at least,*
> *If goodness lead him not, yet weariness*
> *May toss him to my breast.*

Herbert saw well that the strong talents and marvelous abilities of humankind would make us like impatient children, eager to strike out on our own and find our self-made destinies. Only if

God would hold back a sense of full satisfaction from our souls would we search our way back home.

This remains a perennial theological paradox: It is the creative act of God that gives us freedom. Yet, when we use our abilities for our own ends we tend to lose what is best in ourselves and often demean it in others, and push like adolescents away from our spiritual parent. Only if we become restless to find the face of God in some longing for home will we regain a glimpse of our own best faces reflected back toward us in the kindness and smile of God.

Here is where the hunger found in Matthew's story connects with us. We are the people who go out into the wilderness seeking something to give us meaning. And like the crowds in Jesus' day, we lack the resources to take along anything of lasting value. We would die in the wilderness, left to our own devices. As with the crowds around Jesus, there is no food to keep us alive unless God does a miracle. Desire leads us on the quest, but only a miracle of grace will keep us from dying there.

Food is a very big part of our lives. Hunger can be a time clock ticking inside, regulating the hours of our days with calculated passion. Or it can be a biologic need, demanding fuel stops on our restless race. Even more, hunger functions as a psychological drive, forcing us to crave chocolate when we lack love, or driving us to drink, drugs, and sex.

But deeper than all of these things is our search for meaning beyond the drudgery and repetition of our daily activities. It is the spiritual need each person has to know that she is not alone in this gigantic and sometimes unkind maze of life.

Hunger is what the writer of Ecclesiastes meant when he said that God has "set eternity in the hearts of men" (Ecclesiastes 3:11 NIV). Hunger is the pilgrimage of the soul. In other words, the old adage is true: "You are what you eat."

So life beckons us to follow the latest fad, to search for the newest fulfillment, to seek the richest treasure. We consume and devour until we are fed up with life, so to speak, and still we want more.

You are hungry, and you are what you eat. The cravings of your soul will not be stilled. A meal will reset the alarm of your biological clock. Food will keep your hungry body going. Potato chips and a soda will stop the munchies for a while. But what are you feeding your soul?

Augustine reflected on the spiritual character of our race. "Man is one of your creatures, Lord," he said, "and his instinct is to praise you. The thought of you stirs him so deeply that he cannot be content unless he praises you, because you made us for yourself and our hearts find no peace until they rest in you."

What are you eating today? Tomorrow and next week those who are close to you will know whether there was any eternal nourishment in your diet. Amen.

**Proper 14
Pentecost 12
Ordinary Time 19
Matthew 14:22-33**

Ecological Politics

One of the greatest military campaigns ever conducted was the Persian invasion of Greece in 480 BC. King Xerxes (the ruler featured in the pages of the Old Testament book of Esther) set out to redress the humiliation suffered by his father's army at Marathon, where a small Greek force had worn out the massive Persian onslaught and whimpered it into retreat. While the previous force had been huge, Xerxes' collected battalions were massive. Historians who traveled along to document the planned Persian victories claimed that it took seven days for the entire company to pass by any one point.

When the Bosporus waters stalled the entourage, Xerxes commanded his engineers to float a bridge over the gap. But when their temporary pontoon structure was ready, the fickle European weather turned and a grand storm piled up the waters until they swallowed the link.

Xerxes was livid. How dare the god of the deeps challenge him? In a rage, he ordered the waves to be lashed with whips, tied with chains, and sunk beneath the surface. While this may have placated the king, in reality it failed to harm the deeps one whit. They would rise again and again to challenge others who dared to test their uneasy face.

Dangerous Waves In Galilee
Like the disciples of Jesus, out that lonely night on the Sea of Galilee, the storm that rose was a double whammy for them. Only hours before they had been front and center in another of Jesus'

amazing magical acts. The crowds had followed this young rabbi out into the wild places where he was wandering, just to listen and look for miracles.

He certainly gave them a good one — it had been well past mealtime, with no fast-food restaurants in sight when Jesus took the lunch a mother packed for her young son and turned it into a feast that everyone could share. That's when they, Jesus' special deputies, were put in charge of the distribution. No one among the milling men could fail to notice that these fellows were important. They were handpicked agents of this great man, and got to spend all day every day with him. Envy skittered around them as they moved with humble pride to serve these poor folks.

But then Jesus had left them. He had just walked away and gone off into the hills by himself, as if he didn't want to be around them, as if they didn't really matter that much to him. They retaliated and ran from him in the other direction, shoving off across the lake in a boat. Conversation among them, over the waters, must have skittered between rehearsals of their afternoon greatness and pouty uncertainties about Jesus.

They were fisherman, though, and this rowing across Galilee was good therapy. They knew these waters well. Some, like James and John, could probably see the lights in the windows of their parents' home over in Capernaum. Fickle fortunes may challenge them, but they could always come back to the sea. It was their home. They were masters of these acres.

And that's when the second wallop hit them. Their friend, Galilee, rebelled. It caught them by surprise. The winds changed. The horizon melted and sky merged with sea in a toxic soup. They thought they could play this lake like a dance partner, but she kicked them in the shins and was coming back with a kidney punch. They turned the boat into the wind and rowed with passion. They were more than a little scared, even if they wouldn't admit it.

Terror And Tightrope Walking

Then, suddenly, their fear turned up the volume. Like the bow of a ghost ship emerging from a fog bank, something was aiming for them out of the storm. A phantom? Another boat about to be thrown at them by the wicked winds? A premonition of death? They were terrified. And amazed as well, for there was an eerie calmness surrounding this apparition. No waves bounced it, no breezes billowed whatever rags it might own. Swirling about it were the claws of death, but they could neither claim nor impede this water walker.

And certainly it seemed to be striding across the surface, for there was no question now that it was headed toward them. Between gasps of futile rowing and spits to get rid of the spray, they began to make out the form of a man. "It's Jesus!" cried one, and the breathing of their oarsmanship hiccupped. Peter yelled out, "Is it you, my Lord?"

A familiar voice cut through the tempest, as if it were on a different frequency altogether. "It is I! Don't be afraid!"

Things like this don't happen every day, even for disciples of Jesus who are getting used to a winning string of miracles. Surprised by his own giddiness, Peter called out, "Is it really you, my Lord?"

Then, to confirm his passionate boldness, he begged for a chance to find the footing Jesus knew atop the waves. "Come!" commanded Jesus, and Peter stepped gingerly out of the boat.

It was amazing and intriguing to feel the cold softness against his bare feet form in place like a shoe's gel insert. He suddenly had an unusual place to stand!

He tested his left foot against the flood and found he could walk! Gingerly, he shuffled toward Jesus, wondering when he would come to the edge of the wet precipice. But the terra aqua held firm.

Still, the storm had not abated. In fact, it seemed almost as if the wind packed a new punch in its insistence that these strange events not take place. Peter was pummeled by gales that sneaked in from every direction without pattern. He bobbled and turned to beat back his enemy. It was then that his feet slid. The water became slippery, with pockets and holes that no longer supported his footfalls. He felt himself tipping and twisting, and groped the air for non-existent supports. The deep knew his name and was laying claim to his body heel upward.

"Lord, save me!" he cried in panic. And Jesus took his hand. Jesus took his hand and the footing was firm. Jesus took his hand and the waves were tamed. Jesus took his hand and the winds calmed.

They chatted together as if it were a walk in the woods, nothing unusual. Jesus chided his friend for losing focus so quickly, and the two of them stepped into the boat together. Around them the others gaped wordlessly. What do you say when nothing makes sense and yet everything is okay?

More quickly than it had blown in the storm whimpered away. Suddenly the skies were clear, the stars bright, the air fresh and the sea shimmering as it reflected sentinel fires on the shore.

Living With A Story Too Big

What were the disciples to make of this? Nothing, really. You just get on with your life, and tell the tale over drinks every chance you get. For a while at least. But then you begin to hold it and review it and wonder at it. Not so much the freak storm, or even the strange thing Peter did, although, looking back, you wonder how it ever happened. Who, in his right mind, would get out of a boat on a stormy sea and think he could walk on water?

But the recounting of the story would begin to feel weird, as if you were violating some sacred trust. Because you told the story at first out of sheer exhilaration at the experience, and then later because it was such a good story and it made you kind of proud to have been there. But now you know that the story can't be about you. It was always about Jesus. The storm came because Jesus was not there. The winds blew in because the disciples were becoming overconfident in their Superman status. The seas rebelled because, for a moment, everyone and everything had lost focus when Jesus stepped up into the hills by himself. Without Jesus at the center everything becomes dark and brooding and chaotic.

This, then, is why Matthew made sure to tell the story as he did. Not with great embellishments of flair or excitement, but in straightforward simplicity. For the meaning is not to be found in the extraordinary things that occurred, but in the place Jesus must have at the center of every picture.

I think of Madeleine L'Engle's fine story, *Dance in the Desert*. It begins with a caravan of people traveling in hurried fear through a trackless wilderness. They seem to be running from something, and turn furtively to check the movement of shadows at the edge of their peripheral vision. Particularly noticeable among them is a young family, a husband and wife along with their tiny boy.

Night falls and the travelers establish a camp. All gather around the huge bonfire which is lit as a repellent to the darkness and whatever beasts and demons it might hold. From huddled security near the flames, the community shivers at growls and hisses that emanate from the unseen world beyond the licking of the fire. Now and again the piercing reflection of strange eyes looks at them out of the black void and they quickly turn back to comforting small talk which helps them pretend at safety.

But they will not be left alone. The shrieks and warning snarls edge closer. Then a paw appears, or a sniffing nose, only to be withdrawn before spears can poke or arrows be aimed. More fagots are thrown on the fire.

Yet, the beasties and wild things will not be stopped. Growing more daring, a bear steps into their circle and a bold viper slithers in from the other direction. There is panic in the camp as all scatter and leap and search for weapons. In the commotion, the young husband and his younger wife are separated, each believing the other has grabbed their little boy to safety.

But the child was left behind. He faces the wolf and the lion and the bear and the snake and the other wilderness creatures alone. Only there is no distress in his voice, no panic in his cry. Instead, he coos and clucks with delight at these mighty furry and scaly toys that have come to play. He claps his hands and bounces his feet and giggles with animation.

As the caravansary is suddenly pulled from its panicked zigzagging by the tinkle of the child's good humor, all the adults stop and turn, expecting the wild things to tear limb from limb and demolish this human plaything they have abandoned. But it is not so. Instead, the child has brought some kind of intelligent direction to its strange play. His chubby arms are actually orchestrating a symphony of animal cries, and his hands are directing the choreography of a marvelous beastly dance. The bear is on its hind legs, not to swipe and strike but to gyrate with the tempo of the child's clapping. The snakes slither in pairs forming artistic designs in the desert sands. Above, the vultures and hawks swoop and turn and bank and dive in aviary formation. The lions and tigers nod their heads as if in rhythm to celestial instrumentation.

Slowly, and with mesmerizing fascination, the adults creep back to their places by the bonfire. They become the audience in the greatest show on earth. The child whoops and tips and giggles and sways and claps his hands in time with the music of heaven, and the animals of earth dance around him with delight. Even the big people begin to hear transcendent melodies, and the night has become as friendly as dawn or daylight.

Eventually the child tires, as all children do, and the cooing stops, the clapping ceases, and the animals slink away. But they are no longer predators, and the fear of both man and beast has vanished. All that is left is the child. And those who linger in awe know that there is a new center of gravity in the universe.

I cannot reflect back to all of you today what storms and beasts and dark places you are fearing. You know them all too well. They have become, for some of you, a house of horrors from which you would move if you could but you can't. You step out into the weather of each morning wearing a facade of faith and trust, believing you are able again to walk on water. Yet too often, before the day is half finished, and often in full sight of your friends and coworkers traveling with you, you slip and slide and sink.

I do not have any quick-fix solutions for you, no faith waders, no emergency life rafts, or instant pontoons. All I can say is what Matthew, in recounting this story for us, wished to affirm. You've got to keep your attention focused on Jesus, not as an iconic talisman, but as the center of meaning around which everything else begins to revolve and resonate.

At The Center, Jesus

A friend of mine had a wonderful dream some years ago. As he slept, his subconscious imagined him walking along a wide chasm with vertical sides and no means to cross. The footpath was safe enough, but like all of us he was drawn to the edge of the gorge.

Up ahead he noticed a peculiar sight. There seemed to be something yellow billowing just at the overhang of the cliff. Intrigued, he strode ahead to take a better look.

Soon he noticed that it was actually a tent made of yellow fabric. Most fascinating, however, was that it appeared to be hanging in space immediately beyond the limits of terra firma.

As he came close, a man emerged from the tent and greeted him personally, like a dear friend. He knew he recognized the man, but he was unable to remember how or why, or even the man's name. So he played along, fudging his way through a seemingly familiar round of greetings and pleasantries.

The man noticed that my friend was glancing often toward the tent, still amazed at what kind of contraption this might be. "Do you want to try it?" the man asked.

"What do you mean?" my friend responded.

"Well, just come on in," the man said, and stepped into the tent, pulling my friend along.

The floor of the tent was as yellow as the rest, and felt spongy as they went in. My friend dreamt that he was very nervous, and almost pulled back. But the man radiated confidence and drew him along.

As they moved into the tent it bobbed and swayed a bit, and my friend stumbled against his guide. The man steadied him however, and soon my friend got his "sea legs," or whatever it was that one needed to walk easily on this strange surface.

Then they began to fly. My friend didn't know how it was possible, or what propelled the tent along. All he knew is that they were flying and soaring and gliding and sailing. It was awesome.

Quickly my friend lost his fear. Then his curiosity needled him until he had to ask, "How does it fly? What makes it go?"

Instead of answering directly, the man said, "Would you like to try it?"

"What do you mean?" responded my friend.

"Just think about where you would like it to go," came the reply.

So he did. At first there were some jolts and abrupt shifts and dizzying ups and downs, but soon he got the hang of it. They were flying, and he was piloting the tent!

After what felt too short a time but could well have been many dream hours, the man guided the tent back to its place along the cliff. But my friend was not yet ready to relinquish the freedom of the craft, nor his power to control it. So he scuffled with the man, and threw him out onto the cliff. "There!" he cried in victory. "Now I can go wherever I want!"

Immediately, however, the tent began to collapse in on itself and started to plummet into the abyss. No matter how my friend tried to think and force his will on it, the craft dropped like lead.

In spite of his urgent fear my friend knew instantly who the man was. It was Jesus!

"Help me, Jesus!" he cried.

Immediately, Jesus was in the tent with him, and it billowed out and steadied. The fall ended as quickly as it had begun, and they were flying again.

"What happened, Lord?" my friend asked. "Why couldn't I make it go?"

"My child," said Jesus, "didn't you understand that all along I was its energy and its guide? I wanted you to share the flight with me, but it was always propelled along by my will."

So it is wherever we might find ourselves. Unless Jesus is at the center of it all, no craft will convey us along safely. If we try to row the boat without him, all hell eventually breaks loose. But once he comes to us across the waters of our fears, the storms and the beasts are tamed. Amen.

**Proper 15
Pentecost 13
Ordinary Time 20
Matthew 15:(10-20) 21-28**

Religious Balkanization

As a seminary intern in St. Louis, Missouri, I was part of a Jewish-Christian Dialogue group. We were seeking to understand one another's traditions, work together for the good of our neighborhoods, and promote tolerance and respect in society. I had been invited into the group by a member of the church at which I was serving. She grew up Jewish, and in recent years had, in her words, "completed my faith" by gaining an understanding that Jesus is the Messiah foretold by the prophets of Israel.

One of the dimensions of religious life that we all found we had in common across faith traditions and denominational lines was the incessant divisiveness that split our seemingly monolithic communities into dozens of similar yet tenaciously varied subgroups. A Jewish professor of psychology said of his tradition, "If there are ten Jewish males in a city, we create a synagogue. If there are eleven Jewish males, we start thinking about creating a competing synagogue."

A Baptist police officer had a similar tale. He said, "One Baptist family in a neighborhood witnesses until they bring another family to Christ. Then they form a church, and start witnessing to the rest of the community. When another family joins, they have a schism and form a rival church."

According to a Presbyterian homemaker, her communion was a little like vegetable soup. "We have," she said, "the OPs, RPs, BPs, and Split Peas!"

And a Methodist businessman complemented these tales with an apocryphal tale of a man from his faith community who had been shipwrecked for years on a small island. When found by a passing ship, rescuers asked him why he had constructed three huts, since he was there by himself. "Well," he replied, "that one is my home, that one is my church, and that one is my former church."

Religious Bigotry?
Religious life in our world is like that. We call it "Balkanization." The term comes from the history of the Balkan Peninsula in Eastern Europe where centuries of fierce clannish self-preservation have defied the creation of stable broadly encompassing nation states. Large identities, like huge denominations, may expand rapidly for a time, but inevitably splinter groups form and secede, often at the price of vitriolic rhetoric and great emotional pain.

Groups living in an area may have much in common with one another, yet they often become unusually antagonistic in their expressions of contempt for each other. That was certainly the case between the Jews and some of the other communities in the larger Palestinian world of the first century. In Matthew 15, Jesus is confronted by that bias and seems, at first, to buy into it.

Jesus' fame at working miracles has spread, and a woman from the north, beyond mostly Jewish Galilee, has come seeking his favor. She is from Tyre, now part of Lebanon. Her ethnic lineage could have been any of a dozen local varieties, but it is certainly not Jewish. Jesus and his disciples recognize that immediately. When she requests that he heal her daughter, Jesus comes back with the standard segregationist rhetoric announced day by day in the streets and shops and synagogues. "You seek help from someone from your own kind and we'll look after ours."

Did Jesus mean it? Was he as bigoted as all the rest?

There are dozens of other texts that say otherwise. Think of his camaraderie with the Samaritan woman in John 4. Samaritans were even more despised by the Jews than were folks from this woman's background, and Jesus showed no aversion to that woman at all. Or remember Jesus' tenderness with the Roman Centurion (Luke 7) whose servant was dying. Jesus praised the man for his faith, and treated him as a colleague and friend.

A Teaching Moment

So Jesus' initial conversation with this woman is unlikely to have arisen from deep ethnic prejudice on his part. Instead, it seems to have had two targets. First, it appears to be offered for the benefit of Jesus' disciples. They carried with them the attitudes of their day, including the racial paradigms and hierarchies that were taught through marketplace conversations. When Jesus at first voiced their judgments it probably took them by surprise. They knew that Jesus did not limit his behaviors to the conventions of the time in other respects. Furthermore, they were well aware that that Jesus had initiated this journey into a foreign territory, so he must have wanted to be in that setting in the first place.

As they listened to the words emerging from his mouth, the disciples must have cringed a little. Prejudice may feel right in the mind and it may breathe with the bellows of the emotions, but when it is voiced it has a way of losing its rich timbre and echoes tinny and hollow.

I remember a Saturday evening when I was already in bed and the telephone rang. I had often told my elders and ministry staff not to call me after about 8 p.m. on a Saturday evening unless there was a really severe emergency. By that time, my mind was leaning heavily into Sunday morning worship preparations and I needed my rest and sleep in order to be well prepared. Furthermore, we had so often told our daughters that they could not have friends over on Saturday night, and that if they had to be out, to come in quietly so as not to disturb Dad.

But this Saturday night, the phone rang at 11:10. Worried, I rapidly answered it. Our oldest daughter, then a freshman away at college, was on the other end. She was sobbing. My heart clenched. What could have happened? Was she hurt? Did I need to rescue her?

Quickly she assured me that she was not in any danger. Then she asked one of those unanswerable rhetorical questions, "Dad, why do we treat each other the way we do?" She asked it with such passion and vehemence that I knew I needed to wait for a better explanation of her mood, and not too abruptly try to fix things.

She had just gotten back to her residence hall after going to a movie that was shown on campus. It happened to be *American History X,* the biting story of a prejudiced family and the unfolding horror of the way this bigotry destroyed their lives and their communities. The main character kills someone of another race at the beginning, and proudly goes off to jail as a triumphant martyr for the white supremist cause. Flashbacks show how his father indoctrinated ethnic stereotypes and warlike blood pride into the family over mealtime monologues.

But in prison, the only person who defends this tough skinhead against an even crueler world of torment and dehumanization is a black man. Suddenly, the old prejudices lose their punch and moral worlds collide. The inmate gets an education he never expected, and sees color and ethnicity in new ways. He emerges from jail far more reflective, and his boastful prejudices and racial slurs have been virtually wiped clean from his lexography.

Yet, the problem of racism grows tenacious roots in a family or community. When the main character returns, he finds his younger brother welcoming him like a god, ready to fight at his side in the next genetic clash over turf and social dominance. The story winds to a tragic conclusion in which all of the prejudices come back to haunt and bite and disrupt.

So that's the movie my daughter had been viewing. And now, in tears, she needed to talk to me. "Why do we treat each other the way we do?" she asked. What could I say? What would you say? What answer is there to give?

The reality is that we all harbor peevish prejudices, but most of the time we keep them internalized in order to live politically correct lives. What would others think of us if we really told them how we felt about so-and-so or such-and-such? So we parade around in the dignity of refined culture.

Yet, the bigotry remains underneath. And only when it is voiced in all of its ugliness, like my daughter faced from the movie screen, or the disciples of Jesus heard reflected back to them from the uncharacteristic words that shot at this woman, is there the start of a revulsion that may bring healing.

A Test

There is a second reason why Jesus might be using these cruel words, and that is to clarify the issues at stake in this moment of teaching and healing. Jesus is not a magician doing tricks. He is not a spiritual shaman with a few spells in a bag. He is not an itinerant medicine man who fixes up elixirs to sell in a scheming con game.

So it is important that this woman and all who will be part of the aftermath of his healing miracle recognize that Jesus is from Israel; that he is a Jew; that he is appearing in history in a given context that clarifies his identity and mission. Jesus is the Messiah promised by the Hebrew prophets. To ask for his miracles without having that understanding is to play silly religious games which have no purpose. Jesus must be recognized as the one sent by God to turn human history around.

So Jesus' words of challenge to the woman are in part a test. Will she understand that salvation is channeled to the world through Israel? Will she acknowledge that Jesus is more than genie in a bottle for whoever next finds the lamp?

The issue is not so much whether Jesus can deliver on the request given, but whether the request itself matches the true need. On that basis Matthew sets next to one another this story and the preceding short teaching. In verses 10-20 Jesus wrestles with the disciples to identify the values that underlie our actions. Do we act on the basis of external demands, like the peer pressure of the Pharisees in their codes of conduct? Or do we express our actions as the outcome of the values we have internalized?

The latter is more true, Jesus says. Our actions reveal what we have come to believe inside. And because of that, too often in life we get what we deserve. The Pharisees valued a particular kind of religious political correctness, and their behaviors matched. Unfortunately, what they lost in the process was a need for grace. If they could define their own needs and then fulfill those needs through a particular set of actions, there was no longer any room for grace.

Leo Tolstoy wrote a brilliant little story about such desires and the quests they lead us on. He told of a man who had found favor with the governing powers of his society in a Russia now historied, and was allowed to select a parcel of ground as his own possession. The only limitation on this field's size was the requirement that the man be able to plow a furrow around the property in a single day.

Early one morning he set out, drawn by the lure of free land and excited about the small farm he would stake out and claim as his own. He didn't need much, of course — just enough to make a simple living for himself and his family.

By mid-morning he had moved a great distance. Still, when he looked back, the area seemed terribly small. So, since the day was still young, he decided to angle out a bit more. After all, a larger farm would make him a wealthy man. In his mind scenes flashed of his children, robust because of the fine meals they would take off this land. He could see his wife gliding at the ball adorned in a Parisian gown. Men would sidle up to him and seek his opinions; women would giggle with delight as he tipped his hat to them. He was becoming a person of importance!

As noon approached the plowman grew impatient with his slow progress. The circle of land now seemed much too insignificant. He must have more; so once again he widened the sweep of his plow.

Throughout the afternoon he fantasized of kings and princes calling him to court, and the fever for more acres burned in his soul. He plowed with a passion, forgetting to watch the sun as it slipped in the western skies.

Too late he realized that he might not make it back to the starting stake by dusk. In panic, he whipped his horse, pushing at the plow handles as the furrow began to zigzag madly. His heart pounded, his stomach churned and his muscles tightened in desperation. He *must* make it!

But his desire had overextended itself, and inches short of a complete circle he fell to the earth he so desperately coveted, dead of a heart attack. Ironically, wrote Tolstoy, the man was buried on all the land he really needed: a plot of ground three feet by six — a farm for the dead.

We get what we deserve unless we seek grace. The Pharisees plowed their furrow around the field of ritual cleansing, and in that field they themselves would be buried. But this woman knows she has nothing to plow around in order to earn healing for her daughter. She pleads for mercy: just a few crumbs from the master's table.

Whose Table Is It?

Her understanding is more than mere perceptions about herself and what she might or might not have a right to expect; she is also defining the perspective for any reality that surrounds Jesus wherever he goes. No table belongs to those who sit at it. The table is always the master's table. Whoever presumes to own it thereby forfeits a right to draw up a chair or stool.

This brings us back to the religious balkanization nurtured by our ethnic and religious bigotries. When we claim to own the table and determine who we will eat with, the first person to be sent away is Jesus. Think of Matthew's stories again. He tells about the table manners of the Pharisees. They get upset with Jesus. The next thing you know Jesus shows up in Tyre, a foreign nation according to the Pharisees and outside of the care of God. There Jesus has a conversation with an outcast about who gets to eat at the master's table. Wherever Jesus goes, the table is always his. Whoever would approach the table must acknowledge that no child and no dog have a right to eat there. Only those who receive an invitation from the master of the table are welcome. And these invitations are not hard to get. They come freely to those who know who owns the table, and then come seeking grace.

Our participation in the present humanity of this world drives us often toward distinctions, separations, bigotry, and racism — even in the church. That was powerfully brought home to me during our time as missionaries in Nigeria. We were received with openness and love by our friends in the Church of Christ in the Sudan among the Tiv.

But one of their practices really bothered us: on Communion Sunday, everyone was expected to wear white. Now, in itself, wearing white to symbolize purity before God is a great idea. But if a person in those neighborhoods didn't wear white on Communion Sunday, regardless of her spiritual condition, she was physically directed to the back of the church building. And when the loaf and cup of communion were passed, those whose shirts were yellow, or whose skirts had pink designs on otherwise white backgrounds, or those who were too poor to buy a white blouse — these were served the bread and wine last, as if they were second-class citizens in the kingdom or inferior members of the church.

As a bit of a protest, we never wore white on Communion Sunday, and we always sat at the back and received communion last. Even though we were treated nicely enough, we felt the pressures of racism and the horrors of pride and judgment.

That experience taught me the meaning of the old spiritual, "I Got Shoes." While the richly dressed white folks in the old South of the United States marched off to their churches wearing their polished Sunday shoes, the black slaves, with their bare feet, were left to gather for worship as they could. And while white folks were singing about the worldwide church of Christ, black folks were singing:

> *I got shoes! You got shoes! All God's chillun got shoes!*
> *And when de angel Gabriel calls us home, Gonna walk*
> *all over God's heab'n!*

For they knew that God takes care of God's children, and when God brought them finally to glory, God wouldn't check to see the color of their skin, or the whiteness of their clothes, or even the place where they were born. Instead, God would simply ask them if Jesus was their brother. And then, like the only begotten Son, they too would receive a pair of shoes, the sign of people who were no longer barefoot slaves of others but cared-for children of God. Amen.

**Proper 16
Pentecost 14
Ordinary Time 21
Matthew 16:13-20**

Mistaken Identity

Appearances can be deceiving. John Wayne, for instance, acted the part of a genuine cowboy in dozens of motion pictures and fired make-believe rifles and revolvers hundreds of times. Even his last starring role in *The Shootist* had him portray an aging western gunslinger. Yet, here is what Wayne had to say about his skills with a firearm: "I couldn't hit a wall with a six-gun, but I can twirl one. It *looks* good!"

Appearances can be deceiving. Still, we often trust what we see more than what we read or hear. That is one of the reasons why television is so captivating. "Seeing is believing," we say.

Sometimes appearances can even change the way we think about things, and "deceive" us into a whole new attitude. Consider, for example, the report of Dr. Maxwell Maltz, a former New York cosmetic surgeon, who tells of a magazine contest to find the ugliest young woman in the United States. Cruel as such a competition may seem, the magazine editors actually hoped to change the life of this unfortunate person for the better.

Photos poured in from all over North America. The editors selected a young woman with poor features, terrible grooming, and appalling clothes as the "Ugliest Girl in America." For her prize, she won a plane ticket to New York City. There a team of specialists went to work on her. Dr. Maltz reshaped her nose and built up her chin. Others gave her a new hairstyle, an elaborate wardrobe of the latest fashions, and grooming instructions. In a modern Cinderella story, the "ugliest" became quite beautiful almost overnight. Within a few months, she was married.

In fact, says Dr. Maltz, the young woman's whole attitude toward life changed. Before the cosmetic transformation she had been shy and inhibited. She felt foolish and ignorant and out of place in almost any company, but once she had tasted what she could become, her personality also exploded with new possibilities. She became confident and poised, articulate and informed. She attracted people to herself in any crowd.

Appearances can be deceiving. But who among us would be able to say which appearance was the deceptive one — the young woman whose photos won the "Ugliest Girl" contest, or the young woman who waltzed in beauty?

School On The Run
Faith is a matter of appearances as well. It is important that we understand who Jesus is, not just in our sometimes mistaken notions of who we would like him to be, but who he is by his own testimony and actions. That seems to be why Jesus challenges his disciples to read the appearances well as they walk one day in the north country of Palestine. "Who do people say I am?" he asked them.

The setting was quite appropriate for such a question, even if it does not immediately strike us that way from our first reading of the text. They were wandering in the region of Caesarea Philippi, we are told. This was a relatively new city built near the site of an ancient gathering place of spiritual significance on the slopes of Mount Hermon.

Mount Hermon is the highest point in Galilee, a striking conical dormant volcano that provides the only significant ski slopes in modern Israel. Because of its high altitude and its position in the northern regions of the land, Mount Hermon receives more rain on its slopes than do many parts of Palestine. The waters not only run down in creeks and streams, but they also sink below the surface to produce springs on the lower skirts of its foothills.

Near Caesarea Philippi there are springs and streams that create an exceptionally well-watered area. Trees grow in abundance and provide a shaded canopy filled with the sounds of gurgling and trickling waters, and a chorus of bird song. It is no wonder that Jesus would take his disciples there for a strolling Socratic teaching session. But the place held more than just pleasant park-like settings. Because the waters bubbled and gurgled up from caves at the base of the mountain, area residents had long believed this to be the doorway into the underworld. Here, they thought, the spirits of the deep tried to communicate with creatures on the surface. Sometimes sulfuric gasses were emitted, and these only confirmed the presence of otherworldly voices and the breath of Hades.

Over the centuries, a variety of religious sects had used the place as a cultic shrine. They cut niches in the rock walls of the mountain just above the burbling caves and set up statues of gods they thought might be resident there. They even gave the place a spiritual name. They called it the "Gates of Hades." Here, they believed, was the doorway between the realm of the living and the abode of the dead. Those with keen faculties would be able to hear the whispers of the departed and the voice of the underworld gods. It was considered to be a very holy place.

But appearances can be deceiving, so Jesus comes with his disciples to test their perceptions. "Who do people say the Son of Man is?"

We ought not read too much into Jesus' self-identification here. Some think he is making a divine claim already in the question that he asks his disciples. But it is more likely that Jesus is using the term "Son of Man" in a manner similar to that found in the prophecy of Ezekiel. According to Ezekiel, when he was approached by heavenly messengers to form a link in the communication process between God and God's people, the angels called him "Son of Man." The designation was more of a representational term than anything else. In effect it was an acknowledgement that Ezekiel was truly human, but that he was being used in these settings as the conduit between the celestial and the terrestrial.

The "Son of Man," thus, was someone who had no unusual powers in himself, but who had been entrusted with a special revelation that was now supposed to be passed along to others. If

Jesus used the term in this manner, he was merely asking his disciples what people thought about him, now that he had become a point of contact between them and God.

Identity Options: John?
So the answers came. "Some say John the Baptist," they told him. This was Herod's favorite and fearful line. Herod had long been fascinated with Jesus' cousin John, a wild man who lived outside the system. But John was also a prophet who criticized the system and those who ran it, and no one came under more of John's judgmental tirade than did Herod. Herod's forebears had taught him how to survive in politics: it was a matter of deception, bribery, murder, and power plays. When Herod dared to kill his brother and marry his brother's wife, it surprised few. After all, they had been carrying on an openly "secret" affair for years. Moreover, the new alliance produced political benefits for a variety of courtiers and solidified Herod's rule in territorial acquisition and the conferring of titles.

Herod wanted to get rid of John, but he hesitated to kill the man. For one thing, John was a popular figure, and Herod didn't want to build too much resistance. After all, he fancied himself a true "King of the Jews," even if his ethnicity made that a huge stretch, and his religious devotion announced it to be a farce.

Fear of a popular uprising wasn't the only reason Herod didn't want to execute John. Herod was also superstitious enough to believe that John actually spoke for a powerful divinity. So Herod was trying to play it safe. He was not about to garner more ire than necessary, especially if it came from transcendent sources. To have a powerful God against you was an unwise political bargain.

Still, John's public indignation against Herod, especially after Herod stole his brother's wife, was more than the king could tolerate. Herodias, too, disliked the man. She was at least as cunning as her new husband, and would not dismiss John quietly like some quack or minor irritation. Together, they had John put in prison. Even there, however, the prophet refused to be silenced. Herod himself made many secret trips to see the man, now that he was so close at hand. And others who claimed to be John's disciples had ongoing access to their leader through sympathetic guards. The martyr-like John in prison was almost more powerful than was the former wild man of the Jordan valley. His mystique only grew larger.

So Herodias devised a plan to push Herod into the executioner's chair. Using her daughter's beguiling dancing as a lure, she created a scenario where Herod had to buckle. At a heads-of-states banquet where Herod hosted his powerful friends, Herodias got her daughter to serve as entertainment, and then coaxed out of Herod a drunken public promise to reward her seductive whirling in any way she wished. Herod realized too late his wife's part in the plot when it was John the Baptist's head the young woman demanded as payment (Matthew 14:1-12).

Herod followed through on the recompense, for he had made a kingly vow. But since that time he had not slept well, believing that John would come back to haunt him. One may connive and kill others in the royal household, because that is the price of playing with power and living in its vortex. But John was an innocent from outside the system, and there would surely be divine retribution stalking Herod until blood was satisfied with other blood.

So when Jesus showed up looking like John, sounding like John, and running an itinerant school of prophets like John, Herod was sure John had come back to do him in. This new John was probably even more powerful than his previous incarnation — hence the many miracles Herod had heard about — and was probably building a broad base of support to take Herod down in a very painful and public way. Herod believed Jesus was John reborn, and had great reason to fear.

But Jesus wasn't John, and the disciples knew it. They had seen John and Jesus together, and knew the one from the other.

Identity Options: Elijah?

There were other rumors about Jesus' identity floating around, of course. "Elijah" was a favorite among the scribes. They copied scripture and knew it well. Since every manuscript was a handwritten, labor-intensive work of faith, the scribes were committed to knowing every detail of the holy books and transcribing them accurately.

Among the many prophetic notes they painstakingly reproduced was the one left by Malachi. Five hundred years before, when some of the Jews returned from Babylonian exile, three men had stood to communicate God's new challenge to the restored community around Jerusalem. Haggai, the first of the prophetic trio, gave a divine word that was quick and specific. "Build the temple," he shouted to Zerubbabel, "for the Lord your God is with you!" In a few brief motivational speeches on two separate occasions Haggai served as the inspired cheerleader for this ragamuffin crew trying to pretend more strength than they felt in the face of overwhelming circumstances.

Zechariah was the second of the three most recent prophets. By way of apocalyptic visions, Zechariah declared these days to be the harbinger of the end times. With smoke and fire and judgment God would soon come down to destroy all evil and to usher in the glory of the Messianic Age. It would happen right in and around Jerusalem, so those who had recently returned from exile should watch and wait and hope and pray.

The final member of the post-exilic band of prophetic brothers was Malachi. His very name meant "my messenger," so he spoke unabashedly with the voice of God. When Malachi interacted with the crowds of Jerusalem what emerged was a dialogue in which God accused, the people responded with rhetorical questions, and God preached sermons of indignation against them. One of the questions the people asked of God was why God did not return to this temple they had rebuilt? After all, when Solomon created the temple that used to stand here, God showed up at the dedication service and flooded the place with God's own Shekinah glory presence. It was obvious that God had come to live in the temple.

But this time around God didn't seem interested in moving in. An earlier prophet, Ezekiel, had declared visions in which he saw the glory of God leaving Solomon's temple before the Babylonians finally destroyed it. Ezekiel had also predicted that the temple would be rebuilt, and firmly asserted that God's glory presence would re-enter the place. Now the temple was resurrected, however, and still God had not shown up.

Malachi boomed the opinion of God that the people did not really want God in the neighborhood. God would show up when the people were really ready to have God around. As a sign of God's good intentions, intoned Malachi, God would send another messenger to prepare the way. God would raise up Elijah of old, the first of the great prophets, and he would make things ready. Elijah would appear with stern speeches and mighty miracles. The people should get ready, for when Elijah came, God would follow quickly on his heels.

That is why some people thought Jesus was Elijah. Especially among the scribes who copied the prophetic writings this idea took hold. Jesus spoke with divine authority. He performed miraculous healings, just like Elijah had done. Maybe this was the occasion for God to fulfill Malachi's prophecies. If so, Jesus was the new Elijah.

But Jesus' closest disciples knew that was another case of mistaken identity. After all, Jesus had recently spoken clearly about the matter (Matthew 11:14). He said emphatically that John the Baptist was the person that Malachi had written about. John was the new Elijah.

Identity Options: Jeremiah?

So who, then, was Jesus? The disciples reported a couple of other rumors floating about. "Some say you are Jeremiah or one of the other prophets."

Jeremiah was a fitting possibility. More than any of the other prophets, Jeremiah entered scripture with a well-developed personality and a clearly articulated identity. He often reflected introspectively on his divine calling and the painfulness of his vocation. Jeremiah's friend, Baruch, added to the mystique by including biographical information into the record that contained Jeremiah's prophetic tirades.

Moreover, Jeremiah did not disappear from the scene easily. At the end of his prophecies he urged the remnant remaining in Jerusalem to stay there and rebuild. But they were fearful of a return visit from the Babylonian armies, so they kidnapped Jeremiah and forced him to march with them to Egypt. It was at that point that Jeremiah slipped into the hazes of history. Many believed that soon he would recover and roar again out of the fog of time. So when Jesus quoted Jeremiah's prophecy on several occasions, many were quick to pin the ancient seer's name on this new man of God.

Yet, Jesus knew better than anyone else that he was neither John nor Elijah, neither Jeremiah nor another of the prophets come back to life. So he put the matter squarely to those who shared his meals and his snoring and his daily dusty walk, "But who do *you* think I am?"

It was Peter, of course, who answered. Peter is like that boy who sat in the front row of our third grade class. Our teacher would treat us as if we obviously knew what she was talking about. The problem was, we usually didn't. But none of us dared admit our ignorance, believing we would be the butt of every ridicule for the rest of the year.

Not so the boy in the front row. He was already out to lunch in our books and we loved to hate him for it. When our teacher told us things she expected us to know, he would raise his hand and ask her why or what she meant. She would patiently explain everything again more elaborately, and we were in our childhood glory — we got from her what we needed but were too afraid to ask, and we got from our naive classmate someone to razz for being so stupid.

So with Peter. The rest of the disciples don't really know what to say. Can they call Jesus a miracle worker? Should they say he speaks with a prophet's voice? Dare they admit they think he might be Messiah?

All their fears of communication faux pas are put to rest when Peter jumps too quickly into the embarrassing silence and blurts out that Jesus is the Christ, the Son of the living God. But there is no satisfaction here, for the answer is more troubling than the question. As long as Jesus was merely interested in public opinion this discussion was a pleasant way to pass time and share a place in the spotlight of success. But now that Jesus has demanded clarification from them, they cannot hide behind other skirts.

The Familiar Stranger

What should they say? How do you live with someone in the intimacy of the kind of relationship they have had with Jesus and yet linger on the fringes of mistaken identity? As the song put it some years ago:

> *The greatest man I never knew lived just down the hall*
> *And everyday we said hello but never touched at all*
> *He was in his paper, I was in my room*
> *How was I to know he thought I hung the moon*
>
> *The greatest man I never knew came home late every night*
> *He never had too much to say; too much was on his mind*
> *I never really knew him, and now it seems so sad*
> *Everything he gave to us took all he had.*

Jesus is their familiar stranger. He is the man who lives down the hall, yet remains an enigma. The disciples know they don't really know him, yet they are willing to live with the tension as long as nobody has to name it. We are not that different from them.

One of the college courses I often teach is called "Which Jesus?" In it I take my students through Jaroslav Pelikan's book, *Jesus through the Centuries* (Yale, 1999) and the writings of the New Testament, and reflect on the variety of ways in which people think about Jesus. Each time I teach this course, I ask my students to write a paper which requires that they talk with their parents about how Mom and Dad view Jesus. Invariably, I get some papers still wet with tears from students who never before knew the Jesus of their parents' religious devotions. Too long they had passed by one another snickering at the religious folly of others while never having to face the question of Jesus' identity themselves.

Somehow Peter had learned enough during his time as a student in Jesus' rabbinical school to get the answer right on the oral exam. Somehow he managed to sift through the files of mistaken identities and come up with the declaration that Jesus is more than a prophet, more than a religious curiosity, more than a spiritual guru superstar. Jesus is the Christ, the Son of the living God. Jesus brought heaven to earth and earth to heaven. Jesus is the link between imminent and transcendent, and all of us need to know that if we are to get firm footing on the rock that really matters.

With the wall of religious trends there at Caesarea Philippi framed in the background, Jesus affirmed Peter's testimony. None of these other superstitions, commonly known as the "Gates of Hades," spanned the gap between heaven and earth. They never do. We reach and hope and hedge our bets and pray. But unless we know the identity of Jesus, our religious actions are like bad gas burping from the caves of an old volcano.

So the question Jesus asked back then is always relevant. "Who do you say I am?" Do you know? Amen.

**Proper 17
Pentecost 15
Ordinary Time 22
Matthew 16:21-28**

The Road No One Wants To Travel

Some time ago, I was riding a train through central England and a man boarded at one of the stops. As he looked for a seat, he saw my face and beamed at me with great joy. "Hi, Will!" he said brightly, in a wonderful British accent.

Unfortunately, I'm not Will. When he sat next to me and I opened my mouth to protest his mistaken notion of who I was, my flat American English paved the way for his embarrassment. Obviously, I was not the person he expected. Nevertheless, we got along "brilliantly," as the British put it, and I am no longer either Will or a stranger to the man.

Mistaken identity is not all that uncommon, especially when there are only so many variations to our same facial features. After both Albert Schweitzer and Albert Einstein gained worldwide fame, and had their pictures printed in a variety of media, some mistook the former for the latter. Once Schweitzer was approached hesitantly by a mother and daughter duo who asked if he was the great scientist, Einstein. Rather than disappoint them, with more magnanimous grace than he felt, Schweitzer signed an autograph, "Albert Einstein, by way of his friend, Albert Schweitzer."

Or take the case of Queen Elizabeth II of England. She was stopped on one occasion in Norfolk as she entered a tea shop. Two women were exiting carrying baskets of cakes and breads. One commented to her that she looked remarkably similar to the queen. "How very reassuring," said the modest royal personage, and moved on. Her daughter, Princess Anne, had a similar encounter. At a sporting event, she was approached by a woman who said, "Has anyone ever told you that you look like Princess Anne?"

She replied, "I think I'm better looking than she is."

Mistaken identities may be commonplace, but on some occasions they are more serious than others. Certainly that is true in Matthew 16. Just before these verses Jesus had asked his disciples what people were saying about him. Did they get it right? Did they know who he was?

They gave back a variety of answers, and Jesus didn't seem too surprised. But to his disciples' chagrin, neither did he drop the matter there. Instead he pressed the query home in a very personal challenge. "Who do *you* say I am?" he demanded.

There was no room for fudging on this exam. Jesus had made it intense and immediate. No time to go back to the books for a night of cramming.

Fortunately for the others, Peter blurted out an answer: "You are the Christ, the Son of the living God." Fortunately for Peter, he got it right. Jesus praised him on the spot.

Strange Reaction

And that only made this next scene so weird. First, Jesus changed the mood of the conversation too quickly. One moment they were grinning and enjoying that moment when friends reach a new level of insight, commitment, and trust; the next Jesus was rambling on about death and dying. It didn't fit. Peter, certainly, wanted to bask in his celebrity status for a while. After all, he had managed to give the right answer to the toughest, most embarrassing challenge Jesus could have thrown at them. It was like winning an Oscar and a Grammy all at once, and Peter wanted to spend more time at the podium receiving the accolades of both Jesus and the others.

But Jesus steps up to the microphone and starts recording his martyr's testimony. He is going to Jerusalem, he says. He knows his enemies are waiting for him there. He is certain they will arrest him and beat him and make him suffer. And he is confident that the outcome of their actions will result in his death.

There was clearly some kind of incongruity here. Peter had just voiced the great testimony that made Jesus seem invincible. Now, in the next breath, Jesus was breathing defeat and disaster. How do these match up? Where is the connection?

Stranger Response

And if that wasn't enough, things only took a more eerie turn. Peter knew he had to deal with this. After all, Jesus had just identified him as the leader among the twelve. Furthermore, he was still confident about knowing the right answers. So he pulled Jesus aside and started to talk him out of this morbid reflection. "Look here, man; you're scaring us. Do you hear what you're saying? You better get it together, Jesus. This is getting out of hand."

At that moment Jesus roughly pushed Peter away and started shouting at him. "Get away from me, Satan!" he yelled. "You're standing in my way! You're blocking my path! You're fighting against God!"

The disciples were in sudden shock, and Peter most of all. He was so taken aback that he didn't know what to do with himself. What could have caused this sudden tirade?

Everyone stood around for a bit, looking kind of dumb. Then Jesus broke the silence, but with a different demeanor. He poured out his heart. He gave them a sense of what was ahead for him, and for them. And in those moments of conversation Jesus spoke to them about the meaning of life. It is a strange and paradoxical word, but one of the truest things they would ever come to know, and we with them.

Don't Stop Here

For one thing, Jesus told them that life is a journey, not a destination. You see, when Peter made his testimony, his confession, his blubbering statement about who Jesus was, there was a sense of euphoria in the group.

You know how it is. Remember when you first said to someone that you loved her? Remember how those words changed everything? You didn't know if you should say it. You wanted to, but then again, you didn't want to.

But suddenly the words blustered out and smashed into the open space between you. They took over. They stopped the conversation. There was nothing more to be said. You just sat there and looked at one another. It was like time stood still. This is the moment! Make this moment last!

That is what Peter and the others were feeling when he blurted the words for the first time. "We think the world of you, Jesus! You're the Son of God! We love you! We didn't know who we were until you came along!"

When they talk that way, they want to sit around for a while and just smile at each other. The moment was intense and it begged to consume all those in it.

Rabbi Harold Kushner remembered a scene from a television program that he saw years ago. He said it showed a young man and a young woman leaning together against the railing of a ship at sea. The winds tousled at their hair. The sprays showered them now and again. But they didn't notice any of it, because their eyes were glued on each other. The world disappeared around them as they murmured their love.

"If I should die tomorrow," he said softly to her, "I'd have lived an eternity in your love."

She nodded her head in bashful intimacy and leaned over to kiss him. Their lips lingered and they became one as the bustle around them faded. Finally, they slipped away, arm in arm in the waltz of passionate lovers.

Behind them, in the void left as they shuffled, the slow two-step to the left, the camera caught a life preserver hanging on the galley wall. It carried the name of the ship: *Titanic*.

Maybe, in our soap-operish television viewing, that is enough for them: one night of romantic passion. That is the stuff of legends and fairy tales, where everything is compressed to the great hour of heroism or the night of intense love. Prince Charming kisses Sleeping Beauty and everything else gets summarized in a single line: "... and they lived happily ever after." Or the heir to the kingdom finds Cinderella and the rest of the story is just one sentence: "... and they lived happily ever after."

That is often the way we want it, in our books and movies and television programs. We want to linger in the critical moment. We want to feel the emotional high of the kiss in slow motion. We want to sit in the experience of the warm fuzzies and then go get a burger.

But Jesus says, "No." Jesus says that life isn't found in the moment, not even if it is a moment of insight or love or passion. Life is a journey, not a destination.

It is always tempting to settle down into that special moment, though, and try to make it last. When Phil Donahue wrote his autobiography, he told of something that had happened to him decades before, in his early years of broadcasting. He was a reporter for CBS at the time, and they sent him to Holden, West Virginia, in the heart of the Appalachian Mountains. Holden was a coal town where everybody worked the mines. News media were gathering that day because a mine shaft had collapsed trapping 38 men underground.

Rescue teams rushed down as the clock ticked out the anxious limits of human survival. The weather turned bitterly cold. It took three days to clear the passageways and get within striking distance of the ensnared men. Finally, at 2 a.m. on the morning of the fourth day, the first of the desperate miners cleared the surface and stumbled out of the mine entrance.

Families gathered tightly to hug each new survivor. Snow fell over them in the circle of temporary lights as the local pastor called them to huddle around a little fire. He led them in a prayer of thanks for the rescue. Then they held hands and sang "What A Friend We Have In Jesus."

Donahue said it gave him goose bumps. It was *so* beautiful. He told the cameramen to roll the film. But the sub-zero temperatures had frozen the mechanism and they were not able to record anything.

Phil Donahue is not a man to let a golden opportunity to slide by, so he grabbed the pastor aside and asked him to do it all again — the prayer, the song, the spiritual passion. Donahue wanted to make the feelings happen all over again. "We've got 206 television stations across the country," Donahue told him. "Just let us get another camera and you can share this moment of faith with millions."

What happened next astounded the fledgling reporter. The pastor shook his head and said, "Son, I can't do that. We've already prayed to God. We can't do it again. It wouldn't be right."

But that's what Peter wanted, wasn't it? That's what the other disciples desired as well. With Phil Donahue they wished the moment of truth to linger. They craved for the passion to last. They wanted to hold hands and speak kind words and sing those songs of love. They begged for the cameras to roll, and then they hoped to play the video over and over and over again. That's when Jesus reminded them that life is journey, not a destination.

That can be frightening for us because we get used to a moment of great beauty and then want to hold on to that moment. We try again and again to recapture it in some way, and relive it as if it were more real than the rest of our humdrum hours.

It is for that reason that traditions latch onto us. They can become for us reminders of a moment in the past when things seemed so right in our world: a Currier & Ives Christmas, for instance, or an illuminated Thomas Kinkade painting glowing with just the right moment of sunset perfection outside and the warmth of faith and family shining through the windows of a still life home. G. K. Chesterton called tradition "the democracy of the dead." He said that when we fell in love with tradition we handed the current moment over to voices and times from the past. Let them tell us what to do. Let's try to relive the good old days. "The democracy of the dead."

But life is a journey, says Jesus. "If anyone would come after me he must deny himself and take up his cross and follow me."

That means traditions alone cannot keep our faith strong. It means that life and society and the church will always be changing. It can be frightening to us. How often I have had conversations with people who wished to turn back the clock, to put the pages back on the calendar, to relive the past once again. Then everything would be right and good and true and noble.

But it cannot happen. Soren Kierkegaard put it straight when he wrote that if we are really honest, we experience fear when we read these words of Jesus. "Follow me!" he calls. But where? And how? And in what way?

Why can't we just stay in the little huddle, feeling good about ourselves? Why do we have to hit the road with him?

Kierkegaard said that we should really collect up all our New Testaments and bring them out to an open place high on some mountaintop. There we should pile them high and kneel to pray, "God, take this book back again! We can't handle it! It frightens us! And Jesus, go to some other people! Leave us alone!"

Still Jesus stands next to us, sandals on his feet, staff in his hand, and says to us, "Time to go, folks." Life is journey, not a destination, and we know he is right.

Journey With Purpose

There is something more, as well. Jesus tells us that life is a pilgrimage, not a tour.

You know what a tour is, don't you? It's where you let someone else do all the planning. They take care of your luggage. They put you on a big, air-conditioned bus and ferry you around to all the right sights. They pay the entrance fees for your tickets so you don't have to stand in the heat or the sun by the booth. You can stay safe and comfortable and dry, while others do the sweating for you. That's a tour.

When I studied for a semester in Israel, we watched tour groups come through in regular fifteen-minute intervals. We were studying history and archaeology and biblical geography, so we walked and hiked and followed paths that weren't paved. But the tour busses swept by with tourists who saw Palestine from their windows and never breathed the air or felt the wind or sneezed the dust. Clean in, clean out.

A true pilgrimage, however, isn't like that. A pilgrimage is always personal, always firsthand, always something you have to do yourself. That is what Jesus says to his disciples. With Peter they want him to watch God's plans work themselves out from a safe distance. They wish for him to rest with them on the sidelines, to take the tour on the big love boat instead of swimming with sharks.

But Jesus says, "No." Life is a personal journey. He cannot avoid it. He cannot have someone else stand in for him. He has to make the pilgrimage himself.

Walter Wangerin Jr. put it powerfully in his allegory of Jesus as the Ragman. Wangerin pictures himself in a city on a Friday morning. A handsome young man comes to town, dragging behind him a cart made of wood. The cart is piled high with new, clean clothes, bright and shiny and freshly pressed.

Wandering through the streets the trader marches, crying out his strange deal: "Rags! New rags for old! Give me your old rags, your tired rags, your torn, and soiled rags!"

He sees a woman on the back porch of a house. She is old and tired and weary of living. She has a dirty handkerchief pressed to her nose, and she is crying 1,000 tears, sobbing over the pains of her life.

The Ragman takes a clean linen handkerchief from his wagon and brings it to the woman. He lays it across her arm. She blinks at him, wondering what he is up to. Gently the young man opens her fingers and releases the old, dirty, soaking handkerchief from her knotted fist.

Then comes the wonder. The Ragman touches the old rag to his own eyes and begins to weep her tears. Meanwhile, behind him on her porch stands the old woman, tears gone, eyes full of peace.

It happens again. "New rags for old!" he cries, and he comes to a young girl wearing a bloody bandage on her head. He takes the caked and soiled wrap away and gives her a new bonnet from his cart. Then he wraps the old rags around his head. As he does this, the girl's cuts disappear and her skin turns rosy. She dances away with laughter and returns to her friends to play. But the Ragman begins to moan, and from her rags on his head the blood spills down.

He next meets a man. "Do you have a job?" the Ragman asks. With a sneer the man replies, "Are you kidding?" and holds up his shirtsleeve. There is no arm in it. He cannot work. He is disabled.

But the Ragman says, "Give me your shirt. I'll give you mine."

The man's shirt hangs limp as he takes it off, but the Ragman's shirt hangs firm and full because one of the Ragman's arms is still in the sleeve. It goes with the shirt. When the man puts it on, he has a new arm. But the Ragman walks away with one sleeve dangling.

It happens over and over again. The Ragman takes the clothes from the tired, the hurting, the lost, and the lonely. He gathers them to his own body, and takes the pains into his own heart. Then he gives new clothes to new lives with new purpose and new joy.

Finally, around midday, the Ragman finds himself at the center of the city where nothing remains but a stinking garbage heap. It is the accumulated refuse of a society lost to anxiety and torture. On Friday afternoon, the Ragman climbs the hill, stumbling as he drags his cart behind him. He is tired and sore and pained and bleeding. He falls on the wooden beams of the cart, alone and dying from the disease and disaster he has garnered from others.

Wangerin wonders at the sight. In exhaustion and uncertainty he falls asleep. He lies dreaming nightmares through all of Saturday, until he is shaken from his fitful slumbers early on Sunday morning. The ground quakes. Wangerin looks up. In surprise he sees the Ragman stand up. He is alive! The sores are gone, though the scars remain. But the Ragman's clothes are new and clean. Death has been swallowed up and transformed by Life!

Still worn and troubled in his spirit, Wangerin cries up to the Ragman, "Dress me, Ragman! Give me your clothes to wear! Make me new!"

We know the picture. It is the one that Jesus described to the disciples that day on the road. It is an allegory of the pilgrimage he is on, the journey that is always personal, the path that cannot be watched from a distance. Jesus is the Ragman who has to touch lives, who must heal wounds, who is bound by necessity to bring relief. This is the pilgrimage of the Ragman to the center of the city, to the garbage heap of society, to the hill called Golgotha — the Skull! The Place of Death! The Mountain of the Crucifixion! There he must go — personally.

No Spectator Sport

But so, too, those who are with him. Religion is no spectator sport. Harry Emerson Fosdick remembered a storm off the Atlantic coast. A ship foundered on the rocks and the Coast Guard was called out. The captain ordered the lifeboat to be launched, but one of the crew members protested. "Sir," he said in fear, "the wind is offshore and the tide is running out! We can launch the boat, but we'll never get back!"

The captain looked at him with a father's eyes, and then said, "Launch the boat, men. We have to go out. That is our duty. But we don't have to come back."

So it is, in one of the strangest things about life that Jesus tells us here. The one who wants to protect himself, the one who wants to hide herself, the one who wishes to guard himself carefully, will never find the meaning of life. "Whoever wants to save his life will lose it. But whoever loses his life for my sake will find it" (Matthew 16:25 NIV).

That is why Jesus was so angry with Peter. Peter wanted Jesus to take the easy way out. He wanted Jesus to save his own life, to guard his own safety, to keep his body intact. But how could the Ragman not be the Ragman? How could the Son of God not be the Son of God? How could Jesus not do what only he could do?

Do you know what the early church leaders said about Peter? They had a legend about him, and something that happened in his later years. They said that at the time of the great persecution under Nero, the Christians of Rome told Peter to leave. "You're too valuable," they said. "Get out of town! Find your safety! Go to another place and preach the gospel."

According to the legends, Peter is supposed to have gone from the city. Yet only a few days later, Nero had Peter in custody. Soon afterward, he was sent out to die. When the soldiers took Peter to the site of execution, Peter begged of them one last request. He asked that he might be crucified upside down. He said he wasn't worthy to die in the same way as his Lord. So they nailed him to his cross inverted.

Then, according to the stories, the crowds of Christians gathered round. They wanted to be with their beloved leader as he died. "Why," they asked him as he hung there upside down on the cross, "why did you come back, Father Peter? Why did you return to Rome? Why didn't you flee into the hills?"

This is what Peter is supposed to have said. "When you told me to leave the city, I made my escape. But as I was going down the road, I met our Lord Jesus. He was walking back toward Rome, so I asked him, 'Master, where are you going?' He said to me, 'I am going to the city to be crucified.' 'But Lord,' I responded, 'were you not crucified once for all?' And he said to me, 'I saw you fleeing from death and now I wish to be crucified instead of you.' Then I knew what I must do. 'Go, Lord!' I told him. 'I will finish my pilgrimage.' And he said to me, 'Fear not, for I am with you.'"

That is the end of the story for us today. Peter's great confession, Peter's great denial, and Jesus taking both into his great heart, turning them into great grace. Life is a journey, he tells us, not a destination. We cannot sit down at one spot, however lovely it might be, and hug ourselves into some "... happily ever after."

Moreover, life is a pilgrimage, Jesus tells us, not a tour. It is lived in the footsteps of the Master. It is pursued in the purposes of the Ragman and his associates. It is carried out in the mission of the church.

Here is the road no one wants to travel. Yet, if you choose not to walk it, you will never find yourself.

What does this mean for you personally? I don't know. I can't know for you and you can't know for me. But this I do know: I know that you will know what it means for you if Jesus has spoken to you today. Amen.

**Proper 18
Pentecost 16
Ordinary Time 23
Matthew 18:15-20**

Personal Politics

Thomas Browne said that "the vices we scoff at in others laugh at us from within ourselves." More than any other relational failure this is true of hurt and vengeance.

When the great nineteenth-century Spanish General, Ramon Narvaez, lay dying in Madrid, a priest was called in to give him last rites. "Have you forgiven your enemies?" the padre asked.

"Father," confessed Narvaez, "I have no enemies. I shot them all."

Too often that is the story of our lives, and Jesus knows it. Lewis Smedes wrote a book we can hardly step around when thinking about Jesus' words in Matthew 18. Smedes' book is called *Forgive and Forget: Healing the Hurts We Don't Deserve* (HarperSanFrancisco, 1996), and in it he wrestles with us about the commonplace pains we experience in our relationship. One of his stories, based upon true incidents, is about two people he calls Jane and Ralph Graafschap.

Hell Defined

This couple, says Smedes, had been married for more than twenty years. They had three children who had all grown well, and were just in those stages of getting married or leaving for college. Ralph and Jane were about to be empty nesters, and though they loved their offspring, they were secretly anticipating a new time of redeveloping their intimacy as a couple. Jane had given up her personal career goals in order to be a full-time mother and homemaker for these last decades, and she began to plan for reasserting her skills outside their home.

But then tragedy struck. Ralph's younger brother and wife were killed in a horrible car accident. They left three children as orphans, aged eight, ten, and twelve. The community rallied for a short while, providing all kinds of assistance and relief, but Ralph knew that he was the big brother, and to him fell the lot of caring for those kids.

So Ralph and Jane took the three into their home, and Jane started all over again — clothes to buy and clean and mend; groceries to stock for voracious appetites; nighttime cuddling with scared and lonely little ones; Christmases and birthdays to plan for ... Jane's life settled right back into its old routine for another decade.

Ralph was well established in his career, and at the height of his business skills. So he traveled a lot and made deals, and spoke about the sacrifices a family makes when tragedies, like that which happened to his brother, happened. But Jane was left to shuffle three more teenagers through their changing identities and raging hormones. She had hoped to travel some with Ralph, but this new family required all her attentions. Even her biological children were not able to get all the doting they had hoped from their mother as they married and had kids of their own.

By the time nine years had passed, the toll of raising two families had robbed Jane of her vitality and sidelined any chance of another career. Only the youngest of the second tribe was at home, and he was seventeen years old. When he left for college the following fall, Jane would be relieved but emotionally spent. Ralph's rocket had been soaring, however, and Jane couldn't wait to join him for the ride.

That's when Ralph came home from a business trip and broke the news. His secretary, Sue, was a woman of great personality, huge skills, and a lot of good looks. She had made it possible for Ralph to be the man he had become, while Jane was too busy with the children. Sue had time for him. In fact, they traveled often together, something that Jane never seemed to make opportunities for. More than that, Sue absolutely doted on Ralph in a way that he couldn't count on at home. Sue really understood Ralph, while Jane didn't seem to anymore.

Ralph filed for divorce and married Sue. They were both deeply committed Christians, so they joined a church where they could sing and pray and get fed and contribute their considerable skills and money. They were welcomed by the pastor and the leadership team as if God has just sent a wonderful blessing to the church.

Jane, of course, felt cheated on so many fronts. Even in her own church she had become an outsider. Her social life grew very small, and her children didn't know what to do with a single parent. Ralph and Sue were always great fun, but Jane was becoming a bitter tag-along nobody cared to have around.

Ralph was truly a nice guy. Even as he slipped easily into his second marriage, he realized his responsibility before God to make things right with his former wife. So one day he called Jane and told her of his happiness. While he was still a bit unsettled as to the manner in which it had all come about, he could definitely feel God's blessing in all of this. But he also was aware that through the process Jane might have felt hurt at times, so Ralph wanted to ask her forgiveness for whatever pain he might have caused. If Jane could just give Ralph and Sue her blessing, he knew God would be pleased.

What could Jane do? What would you advise her to do? What would you do, if you were in her shoes?

"I want you to bless me," Ralph had said. And before she even knew what she should do, the words spat out of Jane's mouth. "I want you to go to hell!"

"I want you to go to hell." That's really what a relationship that has moved into conflict without forgiveness amounts to, doesn't it? Hell is the place where justice is never tempered by mercy, where relationships are never mended, where grudges grow and grace takes a holiday. Hell is eternity apart from God's forgiving love, and hell is the prison of our unforgiveness into which we lock both our enemies and ourselves with no parole hearings. It's a bit like playing Monopoly and landing on a square that forces you to pick up a card which reads: "GO TO JAIL! GO DIRECTLY TO JAIL! DO NOT PASS GO! DO NOT COLLECT $200!"

Prickly People

Jesus' words to his disciples in Matthew 18 about conflict resolution and forgiveness are wonderful on paper. We read them and nod with understanding and trust. Yet, they are some of the most difficult words of challenge that face us anywhere in scripture.

We've all heard of Gilbert and Sullivan, the dynamic duo of the stage. They created fun-filled musicals and light operas a generation ago, giving high school drama departments and community theaters plenty of material to dazzle and delight. Their names always appeared in tandem on the programs: Gilbert & Sullivan's *H.M.S. Pinafore*; Gilbert & Sullivan's *Patience*; Gilbert & Sullivan's *The Mikado*; Gilbert & Sullivan's *The Pirates of Penzance*.

It was as if they were a married couple. Indeed, much of their career felt like that. It was only right that their names be wedded together in common speech.

At the height of their success, they even purchased a theater together so that they could exert full creative control over their new works. Then came the nasty disagreement. Sullivan ordered the installation of new carpets. But when the bill arrived, Gilbert hit the roof at the cost and refused to share in payment. They argued and fought about it, and finally took the case to court. A legal judgment settled the claim, but it did nothing to heal the breach between them.

These grown men never spoke to one another again as long as they lived. When Sullivan wrote the music for a new production he would mail it to Gilbert. Then, when Gilbert finished the libretto, he would post it back to Sullivan again.

One time they were requested to make a curtain call together. Although they normally refused such things because of their ongoing animosity, this time it was a benefit honoring their joint work, and they couldn't get out of it with grace. So they stayed at opposite sides back stage, entered from the far edges of the curtain, ensured that there were props in between them so that they could not see one another on the platform, and waved in isolation to opposite portions of the gathered audience.

Gilbert quarantined Sullivan in the prison of his mind, and Sullivan banished Gilbert from his social continent. Eventually, they each became warders for the prison of the other. Yet, like the guards who traveled to Australia on the first convict ships, it became apparent all too soon that there was little difference between the jailer and the jailed. Both came ashore onto a deserted island in the middle of an alien sea with no way to escape.

Jesus' words are necessary. We are social creatures who cannot live in isolation. Yet, because of the sin and stupidity that trouble our human condition, we do not live well with those around us. The German philosopher, Schopenhauer, compared us to porcupines trying to nest together on a cold winter's night. We crouch toward one another because we need the heat of other bodies to survive. Yet, the closer we huddle, the more we prick each other with our porcupine quills. And, as Jesus indicates, it is most often those who are closest to us, our "brother" or our "sister," who feel the pain of our presence and we theirs.

Jesus outlines a strategy for addressing our troubled relationships with one another. It is important to follow him down this difficult path in our attempts to restore relational glue to our fractured worlds, for the alternatives are much more destructive.

Keep It Personal

First, Jesus reminds us that we have to make the process of restoration a very personal matter. When we are hurt and when our pride has been damaged, we often become vindictive and belligerent. We charge about and spew venom and seek to build polarized communities of those who are for "us" and against "them." The weapon of response most readily available to us is gossip and rumor. If I can send a toxic word to poison the atmosphere around the person who has hurt me, I hold a new advantage over her or him.

In so doing, of course, I demote the other person from humankind and relegate her or him to animal status or lower. She is no longer my equal; she is a slut or a witch or a bimbo. He has become a pariah or a jackass or a scoundrel.

When my friend becomes my enemy, I feel the need to degrade him or her until they no longer deserve respect and have ceased to be bound with me by the rules of gentlemanly conduct or even the combat and prisoner of war stipulations of the Geneva Convention. Then I can blast them with excessive force and hit below the belt.

After the tragedy of September 11, 2001, our nation experienced something of this intentional projected dehumanization. Those who hijacked the planes, according to many speeches and articles, were not humans, but terrorists. They did not play by the rules. They did not value life as we did. They were schooled in barbarianism. For all these reasons and others like them our nation uttered cries for vengeance, many of which exceeded limits of human respect. It was General Philip Sheridan who gave us the striking reflection in 1869 that "The only good Indian is a dead Indian." Post 9/11 there were many voices that seemed to echo his advice in the new and painful context.

But Jesus demands that we keep our hurting relationship and all its parties personal. "If your brother sins against you go and show him his fault, just between the two of you" (Matthew 18:15 NIV). This instruction strips me of my most destructive weapons and forces me to rehumanize the very one from whom my heart wants to pull away in disgust. Jesus does not claim it will be an easy thing to do. No psychologist would pretend the process is a lark, or carries us along like a carnival ride. Hurt is painful, and so is restoration.

Keep It Communal

Second, Jesus challenges us to keep these matters under the eye of the community. It is hard for us to think communally in our highly individualized societies, yet this is precisely what we need to do. To keep these matters under the eye of the community means to place ourselves in submission to at least some form of group identity. This is not easy. Our consumerist way of life constantly tells us that all of reality revolves around us and our tastes and schedules and desires. In stark contrast, to enter a community means that I give up some of my personal agenda for the sake of the greater good.

We must be absolutely clear here. The Bible never suggests that our individual lives and personalities and desires and actions are of no value. Nor is a complete commitment to communal living the biblical norm. Significantly to the contrary, the scriptures raise high the importance of the individual and the responsibility of the person. In fact, much of economic capitalism, psychological personhood, and political democracy are rooted in and supported by serious reflections on theologies and philosophies drawing on orthodox Christian perspectives.

Yet, our strong obsession with personal rights and self-absorbed experientialism turns our attention too much toward myopic self-interest and away from group dynamics or social interdependence. After years of reflection on the human condition in books like *The People of the Lie* (Touchstone, 1998), *The Different Drum* (Touchstone, 1998), and *The Road Less Traveled* (Touchstone, 2003), M. Scott Peck came to believe that one of the primary maladies of our age is our resistance against community. In his book *A World Waiting to Be Born* (Rider, 1993) he claimed that religious submission was the only cure for the incivility of our age. When we stop being submissive to some form of higher power, he said, we invariably become gods to ourselves and degenerate into a mad world of petty power brokers who are limited only by the striking range of their swinging fists and demanding fingers.

In the church, at least, we must become more aware of what Body Life means. How is it that Jesus has a stake in multiple lives, and what does this mean for our connection to the head of the body? What is the implication of the church's role in multi-ethnic relations for international politics? How do we allow the leadership of the church, empowered by the Spirit and ordained by the community, to speak into the tensions of our lives that disrupt and fracture the fellowship of faith?

There are no easy answers, of course. But Jesus' teaching here demands that we wrestle with the issues. We cannot claim fidelity with God and at the same time play cavalierly in our daily relations with those around us. Each person and each congregation will have to be part of the process of determining how the community and its leadership will invest in reconciliation and restoration.

Thomas Merton, when writing about the religious community with which he spent many years, noted that every prospective participant was initially brought in and made to stand in the center of a circle formed by current members. There he was asked by the abbot, "What do you come seeking?"

The answers varied, of course, in line with the individual's recent experiences. Some said, "I come seeking a deeper relationship with God." Others were more pragmatic: "I desire to become more disciplined in my practices of life." And there were always a few who were simply running away: "I hope to find solace from the world and refuge from the problems that have plagued me."

But Merton said that there was really only one answer which all needed to voice before they could take up residence. "I need mercy!" was the true cry of the heart. "I need mercy!"

Merton said that any other answer betrayed our prideful assertion of self-determination. We wanted, we planned, we were running away from, we desired ... But the person who knew his need of mercy had stepped out of the myopic circle of self-interest long enough to begin to see the fragile interdependence of all who were taken into the larger fellowship of faith. We cannot create community, for it does not revolve around us. We can only enter community or receive it as a gift. Hence, we need mercy in order to walk through its door.

If we know this, then when we experience tension and broken bonds with someone else in the community, it is not ours or theirs to resolve in isolation. The community itself has a stake in all lives and their interactions. Therefore, says Jesus, it is absolutely imperative that we engage the power of the community in addressing the hurts that affect any of its members. Failing to do so does not so much destroy community as it does isolate us from it. We become impoverished when we think we have all the resources to force others into obedience to our way of thinking or living.

Keep It Focused

One more thing that becomes apparent in Jesus' teaching is that the entire emotional content of our relational difficulties needs to be reframed. Jesus says that our goal is to have a brother restored. Moreover, if that does not happen through our own initiatives and those of the community, the outcome must be that we treat the other person in the broken relationship as if he were a "pagan or a tax collector."

These designations sound ominous to us. They are off-putting to our sensibilities of associating with "nice" people. But we need to recall that Jesus was accused of spending too much time with tax collectors and sinners. To treat people in this manner is not to throw stones at them or to turn away in disgust. Rather it is a call to re-engage with them as those whom God is seeking and saving.

When Bill Hybels was a college student in Iowa, he had a roommate who trained his pet dog to growl whenever the town mayor's name was mentioned. No matter what might be happening at any time, if someone happened to say the mayor's name in passing, the little mutt would bristle and growl.

So it is with each of us, when relationships have become strained or undone by someone's carelessness, craft, or calumny. We bristle and growl. In the middle of other conversations, the name might be mentioned and we can feel our stomachs tighten and our breath catch. There is an autonomic response that drives us to pain and frustration.

Only if we can somehow reframe the other person's image in our senses as a "pagan or tax collector" — that is, someone who needs to experience the grace of God — can we still the inner growls and get the beast of our hatred to stop bristling. It is not easy. I have two names in particular that set me off every time I hear them. I wish it were otherwise, but it is not. These people have genuinely hurt me badly in the past, and I carry angst about them into my eternal present.

Yet, I have also learned, over the years, to imagine Jesus standing next to each of them. I have pictured Jesus sitting at table with them, and carrying on conversations of earnest intensity or goodhearted laughter. When I have seen Jesus eating and drinking and sharing the kingdom of God with these two people, the growling of my heart stops, and the menace of bristling disgust or bitterness is tamed.

It is only then that I can hear Jesus saying to me, "You have gained again your sister. You have found again your brother." And something in the world smells sweeter because of it. Amen.

**Proper 19
Pentecost 17
Ordinary Time 24
Matthew 18:21-35**

Political Pardon

My parents were married in the wave of weddings that followed World War II. Dad came home from military operations in Europe to start a new life on the farm, and Mom became his partner in the enterprise. There was only one problem — Dad had an older brother who was destined to take over the family agricultural enterprise, and there was not enough work or income to support two families.

So Dad began to look for other opportunities. For a while he drove a cattle truck, bringing fattened animals to the sales stockyards in south Saint Paul. But then a farming assistant job became available in the neighborhood. There was an older couple with a large farm, and none of their children had decided to stay on to work it. Dad and Mom became the hired help, looking after the animals and the fields, and beginning a family of their own.

In time they became indispensable to the older couple. When senior years caught up with them and they decided to move to a small house in town, Dad and Mom were asked to take up residence in the "big house," and manage the farm as if it was their own. For many years, our family grew up on an agricultural expanse known as "The Evergreen Lane Farm" because of the trees that lined its drive and the sign posted over its entry at the rural gravel road that ran past.

On that farm we learned to play and work and live. We pulled weeds, raised pigs, hauled water, built tree houses, and slathered gallons of red paint on barns and sheds. We settled in there as if we owned the place. But we didn't. Dad and Mom knew all too well that we were sharecroppers. Three-fifths of each harvest belonged to us, but two-fifths went every year to the family that still owned the place. We were never to forget that we only stayed there by their good graces.

By the time I had graduated from high school, changes abounded. Dad had purchased other land, so he now had farming investments of his own. Moreover, my grandparents had retired, and Dad and Mom bought their land as well. And when they moved to the old Brouwer homestead, the land that they had sharecropped for so many years remained under their care as rental property. After all, no one could be trusted more with its well-being than Dad and Mom, who had invested their toil and sweat and family into it for decades. The old sharecropper arrangement was turned into a self-renewing rental contract. If neither the landlord nor my parents said anything by August 1 each summer, the rental arrangement continued for another year.

Even in rural areas, however, things can sometimes change rapidly. Sugar beets as a cash crop were aggressively spreading in the neighborhood, and land prices shot up astronomically. On August 6, one year, the landlord came by to demand more rent. Others would pay it, he said. But Dad rightly pointed out that the rental contract was legally renewed for another year. Perhaps the next spring they should talk about it.

That was the start of six weeks from hell. The landlord demanded more money, but my father remained adamant. Then the landlord started calling at all hours of the day or night, saying nasty things and making strange demands. Since the man was a friend and a neighbor and even an elder in the same rural church of which both families were members, Dad relented and agreed to split the difference with him. It wasn't necessary on Dad's part, since he had a legally binding agreement that would stand up in any court. But good relations were more important to my parents than money, so they thought they would make a concession.

It didn't work. The landlord refused the offer. He had an even higher price in mind, and nothing short of that would be acceptable. He became more and more obnoxious in his demands and dealings. Sometimes he would wait until Dad had gone out into the fields before he would come in his pickup truck and park on the middle of the yard, blowing his horn until Mom went out to talk. Then he would berate her until she was in tears.

That was the limit for Dad. Although he had every right to keep farming that land for another year, and at the rental price prescribed by the contract, he gave it all up. "Go rent your land to someone else," he told the landlord. And the man did.

My parents said very little about it all after the deed was done. They never spoke harshly of the family that had so crassly abused and misused them. It was almost by chance that I later found out that months after the final incident my father went to the landlord's place and asked to talk with him. Dad made the trip to ask forgiveness. Dad told the man that he (my father) had been harboring vengeful thoughts and ill-wishes in his heart, and he requested that the landlord forgive him for wronging him in that way.

Playing the Game

I don't know the outcome of their conversations. All I know is that something inside of me changed when I heard what my father had done. It wasn't even about him or about the deeply emotional respect I had for him. It was more about what life is supposed to be like and how it had glimmered more brightly in that moment. To wrestle anger and bitterness and revenge to the ground and defuse it with grace and mercy and an all-encompassing desire for restored relationships was as strange as it was redemptive.

I thought, of course, of Peter's words to Jesus, "Lord, how many times shall I forgive my brother when he sins against me?"

Peter must have felt pretty good about his request. After all, he went on to suggest extravagant limits: "Up to seven times?"

The wisdom of the day said that forgiveness was a three-times matter. If someone did you a misdeed, it was your obligation before God to forgive him or her. If they were so stupid as to repeat their wrongdoing, you should forgive them again, said the rabbis. After all, it was the God-like thing to do. Even a third expression of magnanimous graciousness was encouraged, because it increased your public esteem and your religious long-suffering character. But there had to be limits on mercy, for justice required its day.

Therefore three times forgiving was the general rule for the truly devout.

So Peter must have felt very good about his inquisitive request, and quite confident that Jesus would commend him for it. Along with the other disciples Peter was well aware of Jesus' less-than-complimentary views about the practices of the religious leaders of the day. If they thought three times of forgiving were enough, Peter doubled it and added one for good measure. This, surely, will resonate with Jesus' high hopes for his followers. A word of praise was certainly about to come.

Needless to say, Peter and those with him were more than taken aback by Jesus' response. "I tell you not seven times, but seventy times seven."

Beyond Numbers

Jesus steps outside of the numbers game and creates a new playing field which is so large that no scores can be kept. In effect, the message Jesus sends is not "You must try harder to learn the discipline of forgiving!" but rather "You must continually remember who you are!" This is what Jesus affirms in the powerful story he next tells.

A man owes an insurmountable debt, says Jesus. His creditor decides to close the books on the account and prosecutes him for failure to pay. At the court hearing the man begs for mercy. Moved by the tragedy of it all, the creditor cancels the debt and gives up his legal actions.

Hardly out of court (and jail) this same man bumps into another fellow who owes him a minor sum. In great belligerence the forgiven man pummels the other into submission. This debtor speaks the same words that his own creditor used a short while before to plead his case in the larger debt settlement: "Be patient with me and I will pay back everything!"

But the newly released debtor feels power surge through his veins. "Not a chance, fellow! You are going to prison until your family can come up with the dough!" And so it happens.

But people are watching. And those who saw what had occurred earlier, when this little bully was treated kindly by his own creditor, report the matter to the one who showed great mercy. He, of course, becomes mightily angry and resumes his legal (and now vindictive) action against the one who refused to show mercy.

Jesus ends his parable with a moral of great force: "This is how my heavenly Father will treat each of you unless you forgive your brother from the heart."

Personal Pain

Several themes emerge from Jesus' story. First, it becomes obvious that forgiveness is always personal because pain is personal. Peter asks about what he should do when his "brother" sins against him. That makes sense to us, even if we don't want to admit it. It is far easier to pretend to deal with people and matters that are at a distance. We can choose to hate terrorists and then choose to talk with politically correct understanding about them because few of us have ever actually been terrorized firsthand. But if a murder has happened in our family, or if a drunk driver has destroyed our property or our health or the life of a loved one, things become highly personal and our glib forgiving spirit runs away.

When Eric Lomax was posted to Singapore in 1941, he knew nothing of the horror that lay ahead of him. With hundreds of other soldiers he was taken captive, and then declared a spy by the Japanese victors. They broke both his arms, smashed several ribs, and left him barely alive. Yet, somehow he survived the death camps and returned home, albeit a damaged man. For fifty years, his seething bitterness poisoned his relationships, first with his father and then with his wife. The former died and the latter divorced him.

In 1985, Lomax received a letter from a former Army chaplain who had made contact with Nagase Takashi, the man who had served as interpreter at Lomax's cruel interrogation. Nagase was deeply offended by his nation's treatment of war prisoners and had devoted the rest of his life to whatever restitution or recompense could be made. He even built a Buddhist temple near the place where Lomax and others had been severely beaten or killed.

Lomax felt the anger of boiling vengeance swell through him. He shared his frustrations with Patti, his second wife. She was indignant that Nagase could write about feeling forgiven and at peace, when she knew the troubles that had dogged her husband for decades. In irritation, she wrote to Nagase about Eric's ongoing emotional pain.

To her surprise, she received a letter of response from Nagase. At first she was almost afraid to open it, but with trembling curiosity she finally relented. What spilled into her lap was "an extraordinarily beautiful letter," as she put it. Even Lomax found himself moved deeply by its compassion and desire for reconciliation.

A year later, Eric and Patti Lomax met Nagase at the location of the famous River Kwai Bridge. In halting English, Nagase repeated, over and over, "I am very, very sorry."

Lomax, in tears, took him by the arm and said, "That's very kind of you to say so."

They met for hours, and Lomax gave Nagase a short letter. In it he said that he could not forget what happened in 1943, but that he had chosen to offer Nagase "total forgiveness." Nagase wept with emotion.

When interviewed later, Lomax said simply, "Sometime the hating has to stop."

There is no end to the hostilities that can erupt between good friends or neighbors or relatives when a slight is incurred or a tragedy can be laid to someone's blame. No end, that is, until someone chooses to say, "Sometime the hating has to stop." That is the very personal moment of forgiveness. It does not come easy. But if we live under the umbrella of God's mercy, it can come.

One-Way Street

A second thing Jesus teaches us in his parable is that forgiveness is essentially one-sided. While we hope for reconciliation — a two-sided outcome — in matters of hurt and broken relationships, forgiveness is not the same thing. Forgiveness is initiated by one party, and is often rebuffed or rejected by the other. That does not undo forgiveness, but it does remind us that forgiveness is essentially one-sided. Forgiveness is what I do or he does or she does. If it leads to mutual restoration, only then does the one-sided forgiveness become two-sided reconciliation.

Jesus emphasizes this in his teaching by showing that when the rich creditor chose to cancel the initial debt, it was neither required nor expected. It happened only because of the choice made by the king. The outcome of the debt cancellation was two-sided, to be sure, but it was initiated as a one-sided movement on the part of the king.

This is a very important point to remember. If we can't have our way in some matter, we often want to make sure that at least the other person can't have her way either. If I hurt, he has to hurt. If I have been wronged, at minimum the other person should be required to make a public show of sorrow. Tit for tat. We want the scales to be balanced somehow, even if it is by way of some kind of mutual expressions that hurt has been caused.

But Jesus is not asking us to be fair people. He is asking that we become excessively unfair in mercy, in the same way that our Father in heaven is merciful with us. It begins as a one-sided initiative.

In February of 1982, Max Lindeman and Harold Wells were sentenced to modest prison terms by a New York judge. Police had booked the pair on rape and assault charges in a highly publicized case. Four months earlier, they had entered a convent in New York City and had brutally victimized a thirty-year-old nun. Not only had they repeatedly raped her, they had also beaten her and then used a nail file to carve 27 crosses into her body. It was a crime which brought even the insensitive to tears.

But when it came time to press charges, the nun refused. She was fully aware that these were the men who attacked her. She did not deny that something evil had happened to her at their hands. Yet, when it came time to overtly accuse the men of their crimes, she chose instead to tell the police and the reporters that, after the model of Jesus, she forgave them. She hoped, she said, that they would learn something from this act of one-sided forgiveness and change their ways.

The police were almost livid. Here were two rotten scoundrels who needed to be punished, yet the nun had tied their hands. Social outrage mounted as the two were tried on lesser charges and jailed for significantly shorter sentences than their basest crimes really demanded.

Did it work? Did the nun's forgiving spirit soften the hearts of Lindeman and Wells? Did they change?

The nun believes that is the wrong question to ask. In her heart, forgiveness works. She is more like Christ, and lives in greater harmony with the Spirit of God than if she had followed through on the requests to press charges.

We cannot know, of course, whether the nun's actions are better or worse for the men or for society generally. We probably could not endure a world where no justice was meted, and where the fabric of social responsibility became a mockery through expectations of convenient, unilateral forgiveness.

Nevertheless, the wisdom of Jesus' words is found precisely in their unusual instruction. Jesus himself would die upon a cross that he did not deserve, and while hanging there would breathe words of divine forgiveness. It is the very contrary nature of forgiveness that requires of us respect. To forgive is an unusual way of life that cuts across our otherwise jaded senses and renegotiates the character of power in our world.

Michael Christopher probed it well in his play *The Black Angel*. He told of Hermann Engel, a German general who was sentenced to thirty years in prison by the Nuremberg court for war crimes. Nearly forgotten by the time he was released, Engel escaped from society and built a small mountain cabin near Alsace to live out his final years in obscurity.

But a journalist named Morrieaux would not let the story die so easily. After all, it had been his village and his family that were destroyed by Engel's brutality. Working carefully by spreading rumors and stirring up old feelings of bitterness, Morrieaux fomented a plot to burn the man's house down around him, and sear him painfully to death.

Even this, though, was not enough. Morrieaux had a thirst for revenge. He wanted to hear a confession from Engel. Then he wanted Engel to understand what was about to happen to him. Morrieaux desired to watch the horror invade Engel's eyes at the moment when his destruction was assured.

So Morrieaux sneaked ahead of the mob he had stirred up; and connived to enter the general's cottage on pretense. But the person he met there was not at all what he expected. There was no gruesomeness about him; he held no monster-like qualities. This was just a feeble old man. In fact, as Morrieaux tried to draw out from him the awful details of his war experiences and crimes, Engel was halting and confused. He could not fully remember all that took place. Dates had blurred and incidents were lost or rewoven.

Morrieaux began to realize that his vengeance would not be sweet, and that the plot he had instigated against the old man was a terrible act of murder. In desperation, he revealed himself and his intentions to Engel, begging that the general escape quickly with him. Even as they spoke there were distant sounds of the mob climbing to do the nasty deed.

Engel finally understood what was going on. But before he would leave with Morrieaux, he required one condition. "What is it?" asked Morrieaux.

"Forgive me," replied Engel.

The journalist was frozen. What should he do?

As the lights come down Morrieaux slipped out of the cottage alone. The mob did its work and the horrible war criminal died. But the journalist remained forever locked in his own prison of unforgiveness.

Forgiveness is a choice, and a unilateral one at that. It cannot go on the bargaining block or it becomes something other than its essential character. Forgiveness is not fair. It is mercy offered, and that act alone sets aside certain demands of justice. It does not negate justice, but it says that a higher power will be entered to trump the ordinary scheme of things for extraordinary purposes.

Growing In Grace

There is a third element of meaning to note in Jesus' teaching parable, and that is that forgiveness is not merely a one-time event, but rather a growing disposition of graciousness. Matthew makes this clear by placing the parable in the middle section of his gospel. Those events leading up to the Transfiguration in chapter 17 show Jesus focusing most of his attention on the crowds who gather around, and emphasizing the character of the kingdom of heaven. Later, following the entry into Jerusalem on Palm Sunday (ch. 21), most of Jesus' teachings will anticipate his death and resurrection and the Messianic Age that these usher in. But here, in between, Jesus spends most of his time with his disciples and tries to help them understand the character of a committed spiritual lifestyle. We call it discipleship.

Jesus makes it clear in his story to Peter that there are others looking on as they practice their piety. It is a group of otherwise undescribed folks who notice how the forgiven debtor treats the man who owes him a little. These people also report the man's actions to the king who had originally laid aside the huge obligation that could never have been paid.

In telling this part of the story, Jesus reminds his disciples and us that the goal of any spiritual formation in our lives is not merely to make us feel good, or to give us a sense of accomplishment. This is quite important, since it was Peter's question that sparked the teaching in the first place. Peter had come asking what it would take for him to know that he had done enough, that he was good enough, that he had arrived as some new level of spiritual graduation.

But accomplishments that become self-serving and occasions for self-congratulations are not the goal of discipleship. Jesus, in fact, had said earlier, in the Sermon on the Mount, that those who pray in public and make a big show of giving to the poor have their immediate gratification, but it holds no heavenly value. The goal of spiritual growth is transformation, not arrival. We are to be engaged in a process whereby we become different people, and through which our world begins to look more and more like the kingdom God intended it to be.

So forgiveness is not merely an act that is repeated on occasion to make us feel good in our accomplishments. Rather, it is a growing disposition of graciousness that is an unfolding process of discipleship identity and lifestyle. Peter ought not to think about how many times he forgives one person or a hundred. Instead, the question is whether his character is continually evolving to become more reflective of God.

Lewis Smedes imported a powerful parable from the Netherlands to illustrate that point. Fouke was the baker in a small Frisian town named Faken. He was a very righteous man. In fact, it seemed often that when he spat out his few words, they sprayed righteousness from his thin lips. He walked with upright dignity, and no one could find a fault in him. Except, maybe, that few found him warm or tender. But then, one does not become as righteous at Fouke by blurring the edges of rigorous spirituality through relational compromises.

Fouke was married to Hilda, and they lived a rigid life of regular hours and faithful church attendance. Fouke carried his Bible prominently in his arm as they strolled with purpose to and from worship services each Sunday, and all could see that this book was well used in between. Fouke was a righteous man, and expected others to be as well.

So it was shatteringly shocking when he came home from the bakery one day to find Hilda in bed with another man. How could she do such a thing? How could she violate their bed? More importantly, how could she tarnish the righteousness of their home, or Fouke's reputation in the community?

Word spread quickly in the small town of Faken, and soon everyone knew that Fouke was about to send away his wife in disgrace. So all were surprised when that didn't happen. Fouke chose, instead, to forgive Hilda and to keep her on as his wife. Fouke made it very clear that he was choosing to forgive Hilda, like the good book said. Everyone knew it, and they commended the baker for his fine show of spiritual depth and mercy.

But Fouke's forgiveness was something he wore like a badge of prideful humility, and never did it actually penetrate his heart of hearts. Not a day went by, but Fouke reminded Hilda of his gracious mercy toward her and how undeserving she was of it. She was a tramp, a hussy, a damaged woman with a weak and willful conscience, and she should be glad that a man of his righteous stature did not get rid of her or hold her to public ridicule.

Every day, Fouke's righteousness and forgiveness sparkled like a cheap bauble that weighed them down like costume jewelry. But in heaven, Fouke's fakery didn't sit well. Every night an angel was sent down to Faken to drop a small pebble into Fouke's heart. In the morning, when he exercised again his righteous vindictiveness, a sharp pain slashed through his body.

Day after day the tiny pebbles accumulated, and the hurting in his chest increased. Before long, tall and upright Fouke began to walk with a bit of a bend, and stoop more when he was working. And his boundless energy seemed sapped by the changes taking place in his body. Within several months Fouke trudged down the street nearly doubled over, and his face wore a constant grimace of pain. In desperation he cried out to God. Surely he did not deserve this! What was happening to him? How could he find relief and release from the awful torment?

That night, an angel was sent to Fouke in Faken. Very patiently the angel told Fouke of the observations that had been made, and the decision to drop a pebble into his heart at every expression of righteous bitterness toward Hilda. By this time, Fouke was in too much pain to protest, or to sputter a declaration of his righteousness over against Hilda's gross waywardness in this sordid matter. All he could do is plead for some way to be healed.

The pebbles could be stopped, he was told, and the pain lessened, if he gained the miracle of Magic Eyes. What might these be, he asked, these Magic Eyes?

The Magic Eyes would allow him to see Hilda as she was before the adultery, Fouke was told. "But you can't change what happened," he protested.

That is true, came the angel's reply. No one, not even God, can change the past. But sometimes the future can be changed. Sometimes hurts can be healed. This is why Fouke needed the Magic Eyes.

"Where do I get them?" he pleaded.

You only need to ask with genuine desire, he was told.

But Fouke was too proud to ask for the Magic Eyes. After all, he was righteous. And besides, Hilda was a guilty woman; why should he look at her in any other way? She was the one who nearly destroyed their marriage. If it were not for righteous Fouke, it could never have been saved.

Yet, day-by-day Fouke's debilitating pain increased, as angels continued to drop pebbles into his heart. By the time he finally relented, he was almost walking on his head, and there was no longer any way to hold himself high and rigid with pride. So, in the dark of night, as a lightening bolt of agony ripped through him, he cried out, "O God, save me!"

The relief didn't happen at once. At least Fouke could not notice any difference for several days. But then life became nuance in little ways. First, through sideways glances from near the floor, Fouke thought that Hilda was looking more pretty. She seemed to have a new glow of beauty emerging from within at times. He couldn't believe it, of course, for the adultery had made her very ugly to him. Yet there it was, and he found himself looking at her more and more often.

Then the critical edge of his chest pains began to subside. After several weeks, he found he could walk with less bend and stand with less stoop. His work at the bakery was easier, of course, but so was his time at home with Hilda. Another month or two went by, and Fouke was walking the streets upright, with a lighthearted step. More importantly, the citizens of Faken noticed that Fouke often took Hilda by the arm, and that there was a genuine warmth between them. Some thought, too, that Fouke's lips were less thin than they used to be, and all were certain that the spray of righteousness had subsided.

No one thought Fouke had become less godly in the process, though. In fact, there was a new aura about him that made people sidle up to him in a way they had never desired before.

Hilda was never sure what had happened to her husband. He never told her about the Magic Eyes. But the way things were turning for them, she didn't need to know.

It makes me wonder though, whether I need those Magic Eyes. How about you? Amen.

**Proper 20
Pentecost 18
Ordinary Time 25
Matthew 20:1-16**

Why Is God Unfair?

One of my favorite courses to teach is "Introduction to Biblical Literature." It is a 200-level course, and therefore only open to upperclassmen. These are college students who have already been around the block once or twice, and they know the rules of the game for getting good grades.

Because the course is a biblical survey, there is a lot of material to cover, and little that can be pursued in depth. Yet, I want my students to think theologically, so I place before the group every year one question that I tell them will be on the final exam. I will ask them to give me some comprehensive ideas for why these writings are collected into the single book we call the Bible, and how this idea weds them together in some form of literary or theological or structural unity.

I tell them that they need to do well on this question above all, and that if they don't give a reasonably appropriate answer, they will not be able to get a high grade for the course. Furthermore, I assure them that I want everyone to pass, and that I would love for all to get an A. To that end, I will help each of them as much as I am able to. They may see me at my office, or correspond with me by way of email. But they must do the work. If they don't do the work, they cannot get the grade.

Sounds reasonable, doesn't it? "You get what you deserve," we say. "He had it coming." "She made her own bed; now she has to lie in it." These are proverbs we use to highlight the fact that ours is a moral universe, and there are causes and effects within the system. More than that, we believe that God made the world in this way, and holds it to certain measures of justice that are not arbitrary.

This Isn't The Way We Like Our Religion

So Jesus' parable at the beginning of Matthew 20 catches us by surprise. The kingdom of heaven is like people working in a vineyard. Some are hired at the crack of dawn, others mid-morning or noon or sometime in the afternoon, and some are even brought to the field just as dusk is setting in. All get paid. But to the chagrin of those who toiled all day, the wage is the same for everybody. No one gets compensated more for greater effort or longer hours. In fact, the inequity of the situation is publicly displayed, for the paymaster deliberately makes a show of giving the late-comers their big bonus in front of all the rest, and then very obviously ignores the extra toil of the strong ones who accomplished more than a dozen times the work of the new guys.

Someone ought to report Jesus to the labor relations board. He either needs to learn a lesson or two in economics, or we would like him to move to another town so he doesn't destroy our lives and livelihoods here.

We have to admit it: According to Jesus' parable, God is unfair. He gives all the same reward regardless of the hours of labor. I remember the stir caused by reports that Jeffrey Dahmer, convicted of so many murders, had become a devout Christian in his short time before execution. There was even a push by some to get his sentence commuted, since he now espoused a faith that changed his behavior and caused him to be sorry for his sins of the past.

That news was greeted with incredulity, of course. Many were suspect of a last-hour conversion. They thought Dahmer was probably trying to manipulate the system in order to save his life. Who wouldn't confess to a little religion if it kept one away from the execution chamber?

But there were others who were indignant on more confessional grounds. Dahmer was a murderer, a deliberate killer who stalked his victims, played with their bodies and their psyches, tortured many of them, and took their lives with cold-blooded calculation before going on to do it all over again. Here is a man (if we can call him that) who showed no remorse and who violated ever humane and moral principle. He does not deserve favor from us or mercy from God. If God grants Jeffrey Dahmer mercy, would we want to be covered under the same umbrella?

For most of us this discussion feels edgy and raw, but it doesn't grab us entirely. We can sit on the sidelines and watch other people debate and wrestle. But I know a family whose daughter lived three blocks from where Jeffrey Dahmer was during much of the time that he was murdering others her age. And I know one family who lost their daughter to a murderer like Dahmer. For them the mercy of God is a matter of serious mishandling if it reaches too far into these lives who brushed up against their own daughters at such a tragic price.

So if we run Jesus' scenario backward, from the point of view of deathbed conversions of criminals and the like, we find the values he espouses even more maddening. More than that, Jesus seems to reward laziness. Some of the folks in his story came early, eager for work and looking for a job. Why should so much attention be paid to the latecomers who couldn't even get up on time in the morning?

But if God is going to reward bad behavior, what is the point of trying hard? Why live as if morals and good behavior are worth anything? What is the point of teaching public piety or instilling values in the younger members of our community? Nobody benefits in the end anyway. All get the same outcome, according to Jesus.

There are some who try to mitigate the differences in lengths of times worked by saying that the latecomers labored with greater diligence than those who were brought to the vineyard early. In the Jerusalem Talmud, there is a very similar story told through the mouth of Rabbi Zeira. He was giving the funeral oration at the premature death of young Rabbi Bun who died when he was 28. This would have been around 300 BC, for Rabbi Bun's father Rabbi Hiyya can be dated to those years.

Rabbi Zeira told a parable about workers on a king's estate who were hired at different times but received the same pay. This was his way of trying to explain the young man's seemingly untimely death. He said that when the workers were presented to the king for payment at the end of the day, all were given the same wage. "We have been working hard all the day, and this one who only labored two hours receives as much salary as we do," the full-day workers complained to the king.

"It is because he has done more in two hours than you in the entire day," came the response.

This, then, fueled Rabbi Zeira's eulogistic homily. "In the same manner [Rabbi Bun], although he had only studied the law up to the age of 28, knew it better than a learned man or a pious man who would have studied it up to the age of 100 years." According to his telling of the parable, the wages are earned appropriately, for the last who were hired worked harder than the first, and accomplished more.

Yet, Jesus won't give us that room for interpretation. He clearly says that the last to be hired have been "idle" all day (Matthew 20:6-7), not just preparing for harder work. No, there is no way that we can make Jesus come out resonating with justice in the telling of this tale.

Even the way in which the pay is handed out at the end of the day is infuriating. Since those who came to work most recently are told to get their reward first, everyone gets to see what it is they earned. And it far exceeds their expectations, since it is the going rate for a full day's work. Talk among the earlier hires is mixed. Some are excited, thinking that this master is incredibly generous, and that they should be making three or six or even ten times as much as these slackers, if their reckoning is correct. Others grow quickly suspicious that the owner of the vineyard is out to lunch at best, or an insensitive fool at worst, as they watch others moving ahead to take exactly what the first were paid. If the guy in charge wanted to deal in several pay scales at least he should be more discreet about it. Because of his open partiality he now has a mad mob forming. The earliest to be hired and last to be paid are ready to revolt and take by force what they believe is coming to them.

This is not a good story, Jesus. It violates our senses and sensibilities!

But maybe we need to read it again. Let's give Jesus the benefit of the doubt and assume that this parable, like his others, is on track with divine wisdom, and that there is another, better interpretation that we miss at first glance.

What Time Of The Day Were You Hired?

Indeed, if you think about it, there is a strangeness about the way that we tend to jump into Jesus' story. We assume quickly that we are part of the group of workers hired early in the day. Maybe that has to do with our years as faithful church members. Maybe we get that from the historic strength of the church in our communities or nation. Maybe we see those who have been objects of our denominational mission efforts as the newbies on the block.

But why should we view it that way? Why do we have this secret suspicion that someone else is getting a better deal than we are? Perhaps Jesus is trying to point that out to us, along with his first listeners. Maybe we need to reposition ourselves in the parable in order to appreciate the character of grace. It may well be that we are the last to arrive, that the Israelites of the Old Testament are the early workers, and that we are getting the good deal called grace.

Are You Getting What You Bargained For?

There is a second thing that is bothersome in the story, if you think about it for a while. Those who were first hired actually bargained for what they received at the end of the day. They do not agree to work for the master of the vineyard until they have put their demands on the table and have sufficiently assured themselves that they will get what they earn, what they think they deserve.

While we may have problems with the lavish graciousness of the master toward those who begin the workday late, we ought also to be a bit queasy about those who make these kinds of deals. In the work places of our lives it is a healthy thing to bargain well for fair wages. But there is something insidious and bordering on evil when other forms of relationship take on measured tones of such justice. Think, for instance, of a child who argues that she or he deserves a bigger allowance because of work done around the house. If all the expenses of that household were assigned in proportion to all the income generated by members of that family, what would a truly fair allowance for a nine-year-old be? In reality, she or he should be working 1,000 lemonade stands just to get food into the kitchen and have a place to sleep.

Once a relationship of trust and love and care is reduced to monetary value, it destroys the fiber of the bond itself. That is why divorce settlements are often so acrimonious. What was begun as a sharing of lives has suddenly devolved into the apportionment of assets. It has to be done, of course, but it violates everything that was taking place when the wedding vows were spoken.

Helmut Thielicke remembered an occasion when that came home to him. He was serving as a hospital chaplain for a time, and noticed the extraordinary care of one particular nurse. She was usually working the night shift, but never used the slower time as a means to slack or loaf. Instead, she was constantly busy, checking every patient on a very regular schedule, and often holding hands with those who were fearful of surgery, praying with the dying, and reading to those who could not sleep for pain or worry.

Thielicke stopped to thank her for her marvelous nursing care. It seemed to make such a difference for those whom he came to visit as a pastor. He asked her if she ever tired of her exhausting hours and often thankless job.

"Not at all," she told him. "In fact, every night I am adding jewels to my crown."

That took him aback, so he asked her what she meant. "Our Lord has promised to reward our good deeds," she replied. "If my tally is correct, I now have 1,374 jewels in my crown in heaven."

Suddenly, wrote Thielicke, he saw her through new eyes. The person he had admired for her inner beauty, tender care, and sacrificial service became in an instant a greedy religious ogre, choosing to locate herself in spots where more heavenly goods could be looted from her unsuspecting prey. It made him sick.

So it should. We only have to remember another story of Jesus, the one we call the prodigal son, to see this crassness reflected back to us in a similar way. There, if you recall, the older brother to the young man who left and squandered his inheritance was irate at the party given when the shiftless fellow returned home. He brazenly reminded their father that he, the more responsible son, had stayed home all these years and had slaved in the fields. Surely he deserved a bigger party and a better piece of the pie than he appeared to be getting.

But his self-centeredness and mercenary spirit were clearly at odds with the character of the Father and the values of the kingdom. So, too, the bargaining that takes place at the beginning of the day in this parable, and then again at the end. "Didn't you bargain for what you got?" the early hires are asked. "Why do you think that is unfair? You are only getting what you thought you were worth." And maybe that is the problem. When we try to mark a service with some value, invariably the price tags never fit.

Who Are You Working For?

There is one other almost deceptively hidden odd point about the story as Jesus tells it. Where is the landowner throughout the tale? It is his estate, his vineyard, and his work that is being done. Yet, he seems to spend most of his time out in the marketplace looking for people. There is a strangeness about his priorities that is at odds with the values driving at least some of the workers. The owner is interested in people and their well-being to a degree not found among the rest. They are good workers, or they are mercenary hires, but they do not have the same care for one another as the master of the estate exhibits.

It is a sobering thought in our consumerist age. Christians are often willing to be classified merely as "church goers," and congregational life in our world is caught up with worship wars and herd-like rushes to the newest and latest and most experiential fads in the next "prevailing" ministry on the block. Church attendance follows value of presentation, so that there is often a direct link between what is given and what is received.

But where is the master of the house in all of this bargaining for better church conditions and greater rewards for service? According to Jesus' tale, he is out in the marketplace looking for those who don't have what it takes to be fully human or fully alive. Maybe it is not so important to God whether we get much out of worship services; maybe we ought to be renegotiating the values of our hearts to see whether our "needs" are tracking with that of the master.

There is something terribly shocking about this parable that alerts us again to the radical meaning of grace. After the initial wonder of our salvation wears off we quickly become merely religious. And in that devolution there is great danger.

No Longer Surprised By Grace?

One college professor presented his class syllabus on the first day of the new semester. He pointed out that there were three papers to be written during the term, and he showed on which days those assignments had to be handed in. He said that these dates were firmly fixed, and that no student should presume that the deadline did not apply to her or him. He asked if the students were clear about this, and all heads nodded.

When the first deadline arrived, all but one student turned in their papers. The one student went to the professor's office and pleaded for more time — just a single day! The student spoke of illness and hardships that had prevented him from completing the assignment, but all the research was finished, and a few more hours would allow the paper to be ready. The professor relented, and granted a one-day extension without penalty. The student was extremely grateful, and sent a note thanking the professor profusely.

When the second deadline arrived, three papers were missing from the pile of student productions. The student who had previously asked for an extension was back, and so were two others with him. As before, all the reasons expressed for failure to complete the assignment were touching and moving and tear-jerking, and the professor again allowed some latitude. The deadline was set aside, and the papers were required by the end of the week. A veritable chorus of praise filled the professor's small office, and blessings were heaped upon him.

When the third due date arrived, the professor was inundated with requests for extensions. Nearly a quarter of the class begged for more time — so many other assignments and tests were due, so many books still needed to be read, so much work was required this late in the semester. But this time the professor held firm. No extensions were to be given. Grades would be marked lower for tardiness. Stunned silence filled the classroom.

The large delegation that met the professor in the hallway near his office was very vocal in their anger. "You can't do this to us! It isn't fair!"

"What isn't fair?" asked the professor. "At the beginning of the term you knew the due date of each paper and you agreed to turn in your work at those times."

"But you let so-and-so have extensions. You can't tell us now that we can't have a few extra days."

"Maybe you are right," said the professor. He opened his grade book and made a rather public subtraction from the grades given to the four former late papers. Each of those students, now also in this group, protested loudly. "You can't do that, Professor! That's not fair!"

"What's not fair?" asked the professor. "Justice or mercy?" The question blanketed them heavily as each student silently slipped away. And the professor? When he reported the incident to others, he simply concluded (paraphrasing Henry Higgins from *My Fair Lady*), "They'd grown accustomed to my grace!"

We grow easily accustomed to God's grace. We need to become "Wow!"ed again by the amazing thing that happens when God chooses to start over in love toward us, even after the "Great Syllabus" demands a divine reckoning.

In her wonderful collection of poetry called, *The Awful Rowing Toward God*, Anne Sexton examines her life like someone in a canoe rowing against the stream of life, encountering hazards along the way, and finally docking at the island of God's home. The concluding poem in the book is called "The Rowing Endeth." In it she sees herself called by God's great laughter to join him for a game of poker. When the cards are dealt, she is surprised and thrilled. She has a royal straight flush. She will trounce God and win for herself whatever prizes God has brought to the table. In great excitement she slaps down her cards, claiming her winnings. Nothing can beat this hand!

But God only laughs, a great, rolling, joyful exuberance that energizes everything around. In rich good humor, with no malice at all, God throws down his cards. Five aces! That's impossible! But there it is. And when Anne loses to God, she knows that really she wins. For God is not stingy with his wealth or his earnings. There are never any losers when they sit at table with God. God's laughter is always without malice or one-upmanship.

This is the gospel according to Jesus' parable. In spite of our good fortunes or savvy playing skills or sheer hard work, we never really win at the game of life when we play it by our own rules. But if God is bending them in the direction of grace, something wonderful always happens. Amen.

**Proper 21
Pentecost 19
Ordinary Time 26
Matthew 21:23-32**

A Career In The Kingdom

When Sadie and Bessie, the famed "Delany Sisters," were in the early years of their second centuries (103 and 105, respectively) they told interviewers, "God only gave you one body, so you better be nice to it. Exercise, because if you don't, by the time you're our age, you'll be pushing up daisies." Fitness gymnasiums ought to put the Delany Sisters on their billboards and quote them into larger profit margins.

Some people get into exercise in a very big way. When Teddy Roosevelt was president of the United States, his exploits at physical endurance were legendary. French diplomat, Jean Jusserand, stationed in Washington DC at the time, developed a good friendship with the president. Teddy often used this friendship to coerce Jusserand into sharing his morning exercise rituals. One day, according to Roosevelt in his autobiography, *Theodore Roosevelt: An Autobiography*, the two of them played several sets of tennis, jogged a number of miles, and then worked out with the medicine ball for an hour. After all of that the president was just getting warmed up, and he asked Jusserand, "What would you like to do now?"

Gasping for breath, Jean replied, "If it's all the same to you, lie down and die!"

Where Did That Come From?

Some people know when enough is enough. Others never seem to quit. For them, tortures like the Hawaiian "Ironman Triathlon" are a happy day — a 2.4 mile swim in the ocean as appetizer, a main course of bicycling for 112 miles, and then a dessert marathon run of 26 miles to finish things off.

Joni Dunn entered the Ironman Triathlon in 1985 at the age of 43, and managed to come in first in her division. Not only that — she set a new record time.

Two things made Joni Dunn's win a real surprise. First, Joni nearly died in a skiing accident a dozen years earlier. She plunged over a cliff and fell more than 100 feet into a deep ravine. Her spine was fractured in seven places and her neck was broken. Joni also suffered several fractures to her head.

At first, doctors held little hope for Joni's survival. She would later remember lying on her hospital bed catching whispers of concerned professional conversation through a blanket of morphine haze. "I heard them say, 'She won't live through the night.' I knew that if I stopped concentrating on living, I would die."

But live she did. It took countless operations to put Joni back together. She emerged from the hospital two inches shorter, and so hunch-backed that when she first saw herself in a mirror she didn't recognize the image.

It was during her long years of therapy that the idea of competing in the Ironman Triathlon began. Still, it took Joni a decade to work up the courage and stamina to enter.

That is the first thing that makes Joni's win in 1985 so surprising — moving from near death to sports endurance triumph. Here is the second — Joni Dunn says that there is only one thing that pulled her through the torture of the grueling race: her religion. "Just moving caused me incredible pain," Joni told her interviewers. "But I knew I had to do this. I come from a very disciplined Dutch Reformed family in Illinois. That discipline has always been with me, and it makes me strong."

That is a surprising testimony, isn't it? Joni Dunn says her religious identity gave her the determination necessary to see her through a life-threatening accident, and then pushed her down the road to win the grueling Ironman Triathlon.

Cafeteria Christianity

Most North American Christians lack such discipline and focus, according to social researcher, Reginald Bibby. His book, *Fragmented Gods* (Ontario, Canada: Irwin, 1987), declared that historic Christianity was all but dead. People today are consumers, he reminded his readers. They go shopping for this and that, a new toy here, a new emotion there, a new sensation each time around. When one pastime doesn't excite them anymore they move on to a new one.

Those same people have become religious consumers in the vast array of church supermarkets, said Bibby. A ritual here, a prayer there, a cause in the next parish, an entertaining preacher on the other side of town, and the Christian population grazes through the cafeteria of weekly specials. Bibby said that most Christians treat religion like a wardrobe — they take different garments out of the closet each Sunday, depending on their spiritual moods, and then they put them all back in the closet on Monday when they take out their "secular" clothes and get on with the real business of life.

Eugene Peterson put it this way in his book, *A Long Obedience* (Westmong, Illinois: InterVarsity, 1980, p. 12): "Religion in our time has been captured by the tourist mindset. Religion is understood as a visit to an attractive site to be made when we have adequate leisure. For some it is a weekly jaunt to church. For others, occasional visits to special services. Some, with a bent for religious entertainment and sacred diversion, plan their lives around special events like retreats, rallies, and conferences.

"We go to see a new personality, to hear a new truth, to get a new experience, and so, somehow, expand our otherwise humdrum lives. The religious life is defined as the latest and the newest: We'll try anything — until something else comes along."

Reviewing Terminology

That is a tragic indictment of our spiritual expressions — particularly so, since the Bible uses two words to describe the character of religion in its truest form, shaped far differently than by either the consumer mindset or the tourist mentality.

The first word is "disciple." This is the term by which the followers of Jesus are known. A disciple is someone who is apprenticed to a master. A disciple is someone who will stick close to him, someone who will follow him through thick and thin, and someone who will not lose energy too quickly, or seek to go his or her own way too soon.

A disciple is a learner, but not in the classroom or a schoolhouse. A disciple is one who follows the master craftsman as he shapes his world. Such an education is not something completed in five hours on an afternoon, or even during a term at college or university. It is something that involves a whole-life commitment, surrounding every motive of our hearts and every choice of our minds. This is what Jesus expected of his relationship with the twelve when he called them to himself as "disciples."

The other word in the Bible for those who take religion seriously is "pilgrim." A pilgrim is someone who is on a journey in life. A pilgrim is someone who has a past in which she is not wallowing, someone who has a present to which he is not tied, and someone who has a future which is not certain, but which is very specific and very real; a future that belongs to God.

When Jesus was questioned by the religious leaders of his day to give credentials for his growing public prominence, he would not comply. It was not because Jesus had no credentials to offer, but because those who were asking for such documents were themselves in no mood to become either disciples or pilgrims. They did not want to submit to religious authorities other than those they believed were already theirs to manipulate. This had become obvious in their interaction with John the Baptist, as Jesus reminded them.

Although this silenced Jesus' would-be accusers, Jesus himself took the matter one step further. He told them a story and then demanded that they explain it for him. Two sons were asked by their father to work the fields. One quickly said, "Yes," but didn't make a move and never stepped out to do the labor. The other was belligerent and immediately refused to be part of his father's livelihood; yet later he realized who he truly was and what he had become, and he then went out to the field to do the work.

What was the point? Jesus' detractors understood quickly that he was speaking about them. It is one thing to parade religious values as high-minded ideals, but quite another thing to put them into practice. No one who refuses to be a disciple can ever become a pilgrim. The disciple gives up his will for the sake of the master's teachings and good graces. The pilgrim sets out on the road of the kingdom in a journey of obedience.

Therein lies the rub, of course, because the wandering steps of pilgrims only reach hallowed ground by first experiencing the bruising of walking too long on the jagged stones of unholy territory. To become a pilgrim means first to become a disciple. Moreover, it requires that one gets to work.

Language Of The Lie

To become this follower of Jesus starts with the sob of a soul that no longer believes the lie of society. We hear the lie every day in its subtle forms: "Things are really getting better and better all the time." "Everyone has an equal opportunity in life." "Education will conquer all our ills." "If you just try hard enough, you can make it on your own."

The advertisements tell us that people are really pretty good, and that the world itself is a rather pleasant and harmless place when we dress right, smell right, eat right, exercise right, and drive the right cars or invest in the right companies. Everything will work out well for the nice people.

Cornelius Plantinga Jr. documented the leaching power of evil well in *Not the Way It's Supposed to Be* (Grand Rapids: Eerdmans, 1995). He called his "breviary of sin" a reflection on life. Like a stranded motorist in the wrong part of town being hustled by ominous turf lords brandishing Saturday night specials, we feel the creeping cancer of a world coming undone.

But the way of the disciple takes its first step with prayer. She cries for help. He confesses that he cannot make it on his own. This was the call and invitation of John the Baptist which too many had refused to heed. From Jesus' perspective, John was the first hint of dawn calling to minds newly awakening from the twisted darkness of the world in which we are trapped: the advertiser who claims to know what I need and what I want and who can make everything better with just a single credit card; the entertainer who promises me a quick fix, a cheap trick, a sensuous fling that really *is* love; the politician who has my best interests at stake, and who will make me ruler with him if I just give him my vote; the psychiatrist who will help me achieve gain without pain by lowering my standards to the mud around me.

Religious Displacement

A disciple sees the world through different eyes and begins the journey of the pilgrim with a cry of repentance. It is the kind of thing one of the psalmists wrote about when confessing that he "dwells in Meshech" (Psalm 120), a place thousands of miles northwest of Jerusalem, somewhere in what we know today as southern Russia.

There was nothing inherently wrong with Meshech as a land. Nor were its people uncontrollably cruel. Instead, within the economy of ancient boundaries, God had placed his people in Palestine for a particular reason. The bridge territory between Africa and Asia, between the deserts of Arabia and the Mediterranean Sea, formed a natural stage on which the drama of divine revelation and redemption could be played. Jerusalem was only a city of the Jebusites until David and God together made it "Zion," the house of the Yahweh. The history of Israel was only a catalogue of tribal squabblings until God chose David and Solomon to create a world-class empire that brought the nations to seek its unusual character.

For the psalmist to decry that he "dwells in Meshech" meant that somewhere along the line he sold out, that he left home, that he boarded the wrong ship and followed a faulty flag. He was the original prodigal son, living in a land where the slur of his dialect brought only stares of alienation. Whether for wealth or adventure, he had stepped down the wrong path long ago, trading his homeland and its covenant with God for a puppet show hitched to deceptive fingers.

Such people have been caught up in the fashions of their day, majoring in minors and having no direction or purpose or real meaning for what they are doing. They find themselves like alcoholics who have been warned by every friend and challenged by every enemy, but remain blind to the dangers of their drinking habits until one morning they struggle awake in an unknown bed, family gone, reputation destroyed, with all their begged and stolen income bargained insanely away for another hangover. "Woe is me!" they cry, in the first note of repentance.

It is then, and then alone, that a ray of hope dawns. The journey begins in that moment, just as Bill W. testified in *The Big Book* of Alcoholics Anonymous. It starts at the bottom.

Cry For Help

The Bible is full of calls for repentance, precisely because none of us will take the journey to God on our own. It is not until we come to our senses, down in the hog wallows of our lives, that we begin to cry in agony for the grace of deliverance. That is the meaning of Jesus' harsh words to those who challenge his authority. They will never know who they are until they first begin with confessions like these:

- Woe is me!
- Too long I have wasted my time in building an empire I cannot keep!
- Too long I have spent my hours in the cult of self-worship, dressing to kill and twisting the lives of others to do my bidding!
- Too long I have wandered in search of myself, only to find that I don't really exist!
- Too long I have lived in a world that will never be home for me!
- Woe is me!

When repentance comes, it can be a devastating thing. I will never forget the torment in my own soul the afternoon that my life collapsed around me and I lay face down on the carpet of a dark room, pounding the floor with my fist, painting my cheeks with my tears, and crying out in the anguish of my soul, "I need you, God! I need you, God! I need you, God!"

It is not the same for everybody, of course. But this I know — I have yet to meet the person in life with true spiritual depth who has not come through some agonizing moment of inner turning: turning from this to that; turning from one set of values to another; turning from lesser gods to Someone far more profound. This, in the Bible, is the meaning of repentance. *Metanoia* is the Greek term. It means the turning of our inner selves from one direction to another.

It is like the old Shaker song:

> *When true simplicity is gained,*
> *To bow and to bend we shan't be ashamed.*
> *To turn, turn will be our delight*
> *Till by turning, turning, we come round right.*

Rattlesnake Blessing

This, obviously, goes against the consumer mentality that has gripped our society. We have been drugged into believing that we are okay on our own, that we have all the means and resources necessary to see us through any jam in life's river. That is why, in a culture guided by consumption, we are not really on the way to anywhere. We do not need to repent, according to pop psychology, but only to obtain. We do not need to change our ways, only our strategies. We do not need some outside power to help us, only to encourage us. We can do just fine on our own, thank you! So Jesus' call to discipleship and pilgrimage often dies before it gets a good response from our lips or a faithful commitment in our actions.

Still, "the longest journey begins with the first step," as the Chinese philosopher, Lao Tzu, put it. And repentance is the first step on the road to healing. Grace has no place in the self-satisfaction of a do-it-yourself religion. Jesus himself said earlier in Matthew's gospel that he did not come to gather the so-called righteous (such as the ones who are satisfied with where they are), but *sinners* to repentance (Matthew 9:12-13).

Some years ago, I heard Madeline L'Engle speaking at a conference. She explained to us how she came, one day, to understand the meaning of her life. At the time she was the "Writer in Residence" at the Cathedral of St. John the Divine on Fifth Avenue in New York City. She met regularly with the rest of the staff at the church, and developed a fast friendship with the Cathedral bishop.

One day, the two of them were talking about the times in their lives when they felt they had grown the most in terms of inner graces and spiritual depth. It did not take long for each to realize that the most creative energies had come to life only at the end of periods of great struggle, often filled with agonizing mental and emotional torment. In fact, said Madeline L'Engle, the best of her books were written just after the worst times of her life!

As they talked, each experienced the growing realization of what poet and hymn-writer, Margaret Clarkson, identified when she penned *Grace Grows Best in Winter* (Grand Rapids: Eerdmans, 1984). More than that, they also found that the turning point leading out of the dark night of the soul was, for each of them, always a moment of repentance.

After some tender moments of further sharing, the bishop got up to leave. At the door, said L'Engle, he stopped for a moment and then turned round to face her. "Madeline," he said to her, "I don't know how to say this, but have a *bad* day!"

He was the best kind of friend, Madeline told us, for he truly cared about her. He did not wish for her to experience the nastiness of life. Yet, he did wish for her to find the grace of God that only emerges with power out of the repentance that comes to those who realize the insufficient, incomplete, inept, and inconsistent state of their hearts. Only a very kind and truly great friend could see that sometimes what we need most is a bad day that will help us turn our hearts toward home.

It reminds me of the story of a cattle rancher who despised religion as something only for wimps. The local pastor had visited him a number of time but got nowhere against the grizzled one's spiritual intransigence. In fact, the last time the preacher had dared approach the ranch house, he had been run off with a shotgun.

The rancher had always taken care of himself. He didn't need any namby-pamby religion stuff to make a go of his life. That is what he taught his three sons, as well.

So the pastor was mighty surprised one day to get an urgent call from the ranch. Could he come out right away and have prayer with Tom, one of the rancher's sons?

Rushing out to the ranch house he found the doctor leaving. "Snakebite," said the doctor. "There's nothing more I can do."

The rancher welcomed the pastor with uncharacteristic warmth and pulled him quickly through the house to a room where Tom was writhing on the bed. "Could you say a prayer for him?" asked the worried father.

He took off his hat, revealing a balding spot the pastor had never seen. Not only that, but he knocked the hats off Dick and Harry, too, standing on the other side of their agonizing brother. And there, in the dimness of that bedroom, the preacher began to pray over Tom: "We thank you, Lord, for sending this rattlesnake to bite Tom, for this is the first time in his life that he has admitted that he needs you. And Lord, we pray for two more rattlesnakes to come along and bite Dick and Harry, so that they, too, might receive this blessing. And then, Lord, we pray for an especially big and ornery cuss of a snake to come along and bite the old man, so that he, too, will know what it means to need you!"

Now, that is probably a prayer we would never dream of praying. Still, the idea is clear. Life begins at death: dying to the trappings of the life around us; dying to the little things that keep us self-absorbed; dying to ourselves in order to find the things that really make us alive. As Jesus put it just a few chapters before this, "What will it profit a man if he gains the whole world, but loses his own soul?" (Matthew 16:26 cf).

Gospel Truth

There is a familiar gospel song that breathes with both the pain and the urgency of Jesus' pleading challenge in these verses. Thomas Dorsey was born in 1899 with music in his soul. He was known as "Georgia Tom," entertainer and blues singer. When he became a Christian, his music took on more depth as Dorsey explored the profound spiritual blues of scripture.

In 1938, Dorsey was scheduled to be the lead singer at a series of revival meetings in St. Louis, Missouri. His wife was pregnant, and Dorsey grew more hesitant to leave her as the due date approached. But she knew the impact of his ministry, and urged her husband to keep his musical commitments for the sake of those who were seeking God. So he traveled the long road from Chicago to St. Louis.

On the first night of the revival, while Dorsey was already on the platform and the service was in progress, a telegram came. Dorsey's wife had died in a sudden and serious childbirth. Dorsey left for Chicago immediately, and found his infant son barely hanging onto life. The child died a few hours later. In a moving funeral service, Thomas Dorsey buried his beloved wife and tiny son in the same casket.

Despondency set in. The great blues singer wandered in a depression that seemed to know no limits. A friend took him in for a while, just to care for his physical needs. One evening, Dorsey wandered over to a piano and began to improvise on the keyboard. A melody gradually emerged, and the words soon followed. It sings in the heart of every person who has started the steps of faith that begin at the point where the resources of self prove insufficient:

> *Precious Lord, take my hand,*
> *Lead me on, help me stand,*
> *I am tired, I am weak, I am worn.*
> *Through the storm, through the night,*
> *Lead me on to the light.*
> *Take my hand, precious Lord; lead me home.*
>
> *When my way grows drear,*
> *Precious Lord, linger near —*
> *When my life is almost gone.*
> *Hear my cry, hear my call,*
> *Hold my hand lest I fall —*
> *Take my hand, precious Lord; lead me home.*

When the darkness appears,
And the night draws near,
And the day is past and gone,
At the river I stand,
Guide my feet, hold my hand,
Take my hand, precious Lord; lead me home.[1]

Amen.

---

1. "Precious Lord, Take My Hand," words and music by Thomas A. Dorsey, 1932.

Proper 22
Pentecost 20
Ordinary Time 27
Matthew 21:33-46

Kingdoms In Conflict

When Vince Lombardi was hired as head coach of the Green Bay Packers in 1958, the team was in dismal shape. A single win in season play the year before had socked the club solidly into the basement of the NFL, and sportscasters everywhere used it as the butt of loser jokes. But Lombardi picked and pulled and prodded and trained and discipled the players into become a winning team. They were NFL champions in three consecutive seasons, and took the game honors for the first two Super Bowls.

Lombardi was a drill sergeant and a strategist, finding and developing the best in each of his players individually and then crafting a team community that could visualize the prize. "Winning isn't everything," he was often quoted as saying, "It's the only thing!" His Packers proved him true, time and again.

Where's The Team?

Coaching is nothing without a team that responds. Leaders are merely overblown egos if there is no one who will follow. During the tumultuous French Revolution of 1789, mobs and madmen rushed through Paris streets. One journalist reported a wide-eyed, wild-haired wastrel lumbering along one day, feverishly demanding from all he saw, "Where is the crowd? I must find them! I am their leader!"

This is the problem Jesus pointedly identifies in his parable. God is the greatest coach, but the team is unwilling to follow. Because of that, people mill about or wander aimlessly. England prior to Churchill was a patchwork of competing ideologies stymied at the crossroads of the twentieth century's critical international events. India before Gandhi lacked cohesive identity and played a game of competitive kowtowing to expatriate authorities, and it was only turned around when he helped inspire a national common cause. Even more tragic is the situation in the kingdom of heaven.

The problem, as Jesus' story puts it, is that the great leader has come — twice over, in fact — but those who are sub-coaches think they can play the game without a head coach. They use a different playbook and try to win minor trophies that will gather dust on their mantles, rather than looking for the winning season that would honor the owner.

Quick History Lesson

Jesus' short story mirrors the vast sweep of biblical theology, and frames it in the strong political language that opens the Pentateuch. In the world of the Bible, Genesis functions as the prologue to the covenant God makes with Israel at Mount Sinai (Exodus 20-24). Modeled after the Suzerain-Vassal covenants widely used in that day to organize affairs between kings and subjects, these covenants had standardized parts. The prologue rehearsed the background to the making of the covenant, and gave reasons why it was necessary. Thus Genesis was built, literally, in four major sections that each helped ancient Israel understand a portion of the historical necessity that brought about this treaty ratification. Chapters 1-11 told of the good world God created and also the nasty civil war that threatened to destroy it. Chapters 12-25 spoke of Abraham and the way that God selected him to head the team which would become the advance troops in taking back God's world from the evil intruders. Chapters 26-36 are a character study of how Jacob became "Israel" (one who struggles with God) and thus bequeathed the nation with a name and an identity. Finally, Genesis 37-50 focused on Joseph, and described how the nation eventually wound up in Egypt, from which it had so recently emerged. The result was a new and winning team that would form God's estate among the rest of the nations of the world. This is the picture Jesus presents in summary form in his parable.

In Israel's world there were three kinds of covenants regularly made. The first was a "Parity Agreement" which shaped relations between individuals of similar social rank in the ancient world (think of Jacob and Laban forming their parity treaty at the end of Genesis 31). In addition there were two varieties of king-subject covenants. One was a "Royal Grant." This was essentially a gift bestowed by a person of power and political privilege upon someone down-caste a rung or more. Usually the king noticed an act of bravery in battle, or striking beauty in the ballroom, or uncommon beneficence in bearing, and gave a gift in public recognition. One obvious example is that of Persian king, Xerxes, honoring Mordecai in the story of Esther (chs. 3-6). The Royal Grant was always a one-way act, with no specific reciprocal deed required.

The second type of king-subject covenant was known as the "Suzerain-Vassal Treaty." It was quite different from the Royal Grant. It moved on a two-way street, with both parties giving and expecting much. When a Suzerain-Vassal Treaty was ratified, kings would provide safety and food and shelter and relief and community building grants, while the people were obligated to pay taxes, offer troops for the regiments, send food supplies, and enlist in government work projects. Rather than merely a bequest awarded by one to the other as was true with the Royal Grant, the Suzerain-Vassal treaty ensured that both parties invest in the relationship.

Interestingly, in the series of covenants developed between God and Abram in Genesis 12-17, the first three (Genesis 12, 13, 15) appear to be "Royal Grants." Each time a gift is proffered — land (twice) and a biological heir who will help establish a great Abram-family nation. Strikingly, after each Royal Grant is spoken, Abram seems to lose confidence in the gift. Rather than stay in the land of promise, he runs to Egypt to find better grazing for his crops and food sources for his crew. Similarly, instead of mating again with wife Sarai to realize a biological heir, Abram and the younger Hagar bond to produce Ishmael. Three times God makes Royal Grants with Abram, and each time Abram takes matters into his own hands.

In the fourth covenant ceremony in Genesis 17, however, God changed tactics, and Abram came out of the deal with a transformed heart. There God established a Suzerain-Vassal covenant.

In it God promised land and blessings and descendents, but God also called Abram to respond with faith and fealty. Abram was not merely the target of a nice gift; he was now called to share the mind and the mission of the Maker. God declared name changes for Abram and Sarai, and also required the act of circumcision which would publicly mark all the males of the family as "owned" by God.

The outcome to this fourth covenant-making event was strikingly different than that following the previous three. Most notably, when pushed to the limit of trust in Genesis 22, the new Abraham gave evidence that his covenant relationship with God superseded all other loyalties and commitments. Because of the Suzerain-Vassal covenant established in Genesis 17, faith stuck deeply in Abraham's life.

Of course, for the Israelites at Mount Sinai who reviewed this history, the lesson was clear. God's gifts alone do not bind us into God's redemptive enterprises. A faith response and loyal service round out the picture. Without investment on our part, no great blessing of God lingers for our enjoyment. Abraham and his descendents form a great team because they have a great coach who gives the right incentives and demands the right stuff in return.

This is the plot underlying Jesus' words in the parable of the tenants. Israel was blessed by God to share in the divine enterprise of making the garden come alive on planet earth. Unfortunately, too many of the leaders among the people had other ideas, and set themselves up as alternative kings, thinking they could divert the treasures of the kingdom into their own bank accounts. The result was the religious confusion that plagued Israel throughout its later history. Even the prophets could not steer the nation back to obedience and trust for the original great coach and leader.

Whose Fault Is It?

Abbott and Costello entranced an earlier generation with their sidesplitting routine "Who's on First." Pretending to discuss the players of a baseball team, names were confused with positions until tracking the game became an exercise in futility.

Among the religious discussions of Jesus' day, there was a similar confusion of identities. For some, evil was inherent in the system like yin's twin yang. For others, humans had incurred the wrath of the gods and were punished through the spread of vices that flowed out of Pandora's mythical box. Others still believed divine perfection was trapped by a mean-spirited creator into the corrupt and forgetful stuff of human flesh, waiting magical gnostic liberation.

Jesus' design in his sweeping tale is to give a different view of the origins of evil. God is good; creation is good; and human alienation from the good is a late introduction brought about by our sinful choices. For Jesus' audience of religious leaders, the message communicated was that all of humanity had the same opportunities to remain in fellowship with the creator, and all are equally responsible for their distance from God.

But Jesus also couched the story in swaddling folds of never-ending grace. Time after time God initiated a restoration of relationships with humanity. All are welcome to be part of the team. As part of our latter days, in fact, God sent in Jesus to spur the team to new spiritual victories. Jesus is the expression of God's righteousness inserted recently into our world, and the means by which we are attached to the righteous endeavors of God. He is the glue that binds the team together and keeps them connected both to the owner and the game.

By this time, according to Matthew, Jesus has clearly expressed his divine power and wisdom. Enough so, in fact, that he can begin to speak about the sacrificial death toward which he is heading. In these verses he almost shouts out what is about to happen, hoping to shock us into spiritual recovery in a kind of critical intervention. Winning, for Jesus, means playing by a set of rules that has not been used for a long time on planet earth. It is like the "deep magic" of Aslan in C. S. Lewis' great tale, *The Lion, the Witch, and the Wardrobe*. Most don't understand it, but without it the game becomes a never-ending cycle of violence in which there are only losers.

Forging A New Team

For that reason Jesus gives a brief exhortation about the characteristics that mark those on his team. It is not self-preservation but service that counts. It is not superiority but selflessness that wins points. It is not stridency but sacrifice that finds recognition from the owner of the club. Jesus is building a team that will change the world. Unfortunately, on that day, too few people seemed willing to show up at the try-outs.

There is a scene in Tolkien's *The Fellowship of the Ring*, where a partnership is forged among those who would accompany Frodo on his journey to destroy the ring of power. The movie version makes for a very gripping visual illustration, and the original literary text is equally as moving. What comes through is a sense of selflessness as the bond that unites these creatures. Furthermore, each subsumes his will to the greater cause, and trusts an unseen and transcendent good for an outcome that will bless all of Middle Earth, even if the trek itself causes the demise of any or all of the compatriots.

So it is in Jesus' small glimpse of the mission of God. In a world turned cold to its creator, in an age riddled by Delphic oracles and temple prostitutes and emperors claiming divinity, in a little corner of geography where messianic hopes ran high, God called together a strange team to make its mark by playing a different game.

Walter Wangerin Jr., in his great allegory, *The Book of the Dun Cow* (along with its wonderful sequel, *The Book of Sorrows*), captures both the scope of the divine mission as well as the underrated character of the team. If the focus remains on the team apart from the mission, the point is lost. God is reclaiming God's creation, but does so through human agency. The game is fierce and the playing field is rough. Only those who can tear up their personal score sheets in order get into God's game will make the team. Only they are truly called. Only they are equipped to serve and follow and play on the greatest winning team of all time.

Jesus is on the road to the cross, and he calls others to join him in that pilgrimage. The cost of discipleship, as Dietrich Bonhoeffer noted in his book, *The Cost of Discipleship*, is self-denial, and Jesus' words are a strong call to that vocation, not as an end in itself or as a means to a self-help goal (like dieting), but rather as a counter-cultural missional testimony. Those who travel this road do not get to Easter without first enduring Good Friday; they do not presume a glorious outcome that gathers the media like paparazzi vultures, but sense that the journey of service brings light in darkness, hope in despair, healing for pain, and faith where power corrupts and destroys.

Have you entered the cause? Amen.